The Self-Directed Learning Handbook

The Self-Directed Learning Handbook

Challenging
Adolescent Students
to Excel

Maurice Gibbons

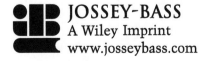
JOSSEY-BASS
A Wiley Imprint
www.josseybass.com

Published by Jossey-Bass
A Wiley Imprint
989 Market Street, San Francisco, CA 94103-1741   www.josseybass.com

Resources B, E, and G in this book may be reproduced for educational/training activities. We do, however, require that the following statement appear on all reproductions:

The Self-Directed Learning Handbook by Maurice Gibbons.
Copyright © 2002 by John Wiley & Sons, Inc.

This free permission is limited to the reproduction of material for educational/training events. Systematic or large-scale reproduction or distribution (more than one hundred copies per year)—or inclusion of items in publications for sale—may be done only with prior written permission. Also, reproduction on computer disk or by any other electronic means requires prior written permission. Requests to the Publisher for permission should be addressed to the Permissions Department, John Wiley & Sons, Inc., 111 River Street, Hoboken, NJ 07030, (201) 748-6011, fax (201) 748-6008, e-mail: permcoordinator@wiley.com.

Jossey-Bass books and products are available through most bookstores. To contact Jossey-Bass directly, call our Customer Care Department within the U.S. at 800-956-7739, outside the U.S. at 317-572-3993 or fax 317-572-4002.

Jossey-Bass also publishes its books in a variety of electronic formats. Some content that appears in print may not be available in electronic books.

Library of Congress Cataloging-in-Publication Data

Gibbons, Maurice, date–
    The self-directed learning handbook: challenging adolescent students to excel/Maurice Gibbons.—1st ed.
        p. cm.— (The Jossey-Bass education series)
    Includes bibliographical references and index.
    ISBN 0-7879-5955-3 (pbk.: alk. paper)
    1. Individualized instruction—Handbooks, manuals, etc. 2. Independent study—Handbooks, manuals, etc. 3. Self-culture—Handbooks, manuals, etc. 4. Middle school teaching—Handbooks, manuals, etc. 5. High school teaching—Handbooks, manuals, etc. I. Title. II. Series.
LB1031.G53 2002
371.39'4—dc21
                                                                                            2002012169

All that hinders the individual from expressing the full power of the infinite universe is his lack of faith, his inability to realize the stupendous truth that he himself is the very power which he seeks.

—The last entry in my father's journal

Contents

Preface   xiii

Acknowledgments   xvii

1   The Case for Self-Directed Learning   1

    What Is Self-Directed Learning?   2

    How Does Research Support SDL?   6

    The Major Principles of an SDL Program   9

    The Essential Elements of SDL   11

    Approaching SDL in Stages   13

2   A Framework for Teaching SDL   14

    Defining the Course   15

    Expanding Learning Options and Environments   16

    Building Independent Thinking Skills   18

    Negotiating Student Learning Agreements   20

    Establishing Assessment Processes   21

3   Rethinking Student Coursework   23

    Essential Planning Steps   23

    Understanding the Stages of SDL   24

    Linking the Stages to Grade Levels   28

    Designating Course Outcomes   29

    Developing Self-Managed Course Units   34

    Student-Planned Coursework and Projects   38

    Focusing on Competencies and Challenges   39

4   Planning Lessons and Projects   **43**

   Principles for Planning Lessons   43

   Designing Learning Episodes   46

   Creating Experiences   47

   Promoting Study   49

   Encouraging Productivity   51

   Involving Students in Project Planning   52

5   Teaching Independent Thinking   **57**

   Inviting Inquiry and Initiative   58

   Developing Problem-Solving Skills   64

   Using Process Frameworks: Investigation and Action   65

   Cultivating Process Thinking and Attitudes   68

6   Negotiating Student Learning Agreements   **73**

   The Learning Agreement or Contract   73

   The Elements of a Contract   74

   Negotiating Contract Agreements   81

   Sample Contracts   87

   Tracking Student Progress   90

7   Motivating and Empowering Students   **93**

   Encouraging Students to Pursue SDL   93

   Motivating Students to Motivate Themselves   95

   The Working Journal as a Motivational Tool   99

   Dealing with the SDL Crisis   101

   Working with Difficult Students   106

8   Assessing Student Achievement   **110**

   Promoting Student Self-Assessment   111

   Assessing General Skills   113

   Assessing Coursework   113

   Evaluating Projects and Assignments   119

   Portfolios for Personal Learning   121

   Passage and Graduation Criteria   122

   Demonstrations, Celebrations, and Conferences   126

9   Pursuing a Path of Excellence   **132**

   The Teacher Is the Key Person   132

   Making a Difference to the Student   135

Starting an SDL School   137

Administrative Support for SDL   138

Creating a Shared Vision   140

Resource A: How Much SDL Are You Teaching Now?   142

Resource B: How Self-Directing Are You?   144
A Self-Assessment Instrument

Resource C: The Passage Process   148

Resource D: The Integrated SDL Unit: The Kinds of   152
Activities Involved

Resource E: Inner States for SDL   154

Resource F: Sample Process Templates   157

Resource G: Guidelines, Traps, and Boosters   159

Resource H: The Support Group or Triad   163

Resource I: Samples from a Student's Working Journal   166

Resource J: Some of the Many Ways Students Can Learn   170

Bibliography   172

Index   177

The Author   183

Preface

FEW PROFESSIONS are as rewarding as teaching, and no other profession is as important, especially now that school is the single remaining stable influence in students' lives. This book is for teachers seeking new ways to engage adolescent students and to prepare them for a successful life of learning and achievement. It is for those who are ready to open a new range of learning opportunities to students and a new repertoire of skills that will both empower them and compel them to action. This book is about teaching middle and high school students to find their own direction in learning and to develop skilful ways of getting to the challenging goals they choose.

As a beginning elementary school teacher, I was struck by the difficulty of teaching one program to a class of very diverse students. How could I provide every student with a fair opportunity to learn and progress? I began to individualize, sending some students off to learn on their own and others to do basic work in the subject with a talented classmate while I taught the middle group. The class often operated as a one-room country school, with different groups doing different things and everyone helping everyone else. It looked and felt like a learning community.

When I moved to teaching high school, I carried the same concerns and found even greater diversity among students and a more intense focus on covering the program. As a beginning teacher, I was given a healthy sampling of the most difficult students to teach. Working with them, I soon discovered that the onset of adolescence raises many new issues. Students enter the hormonal storm, they begin to define their individual identities, they face value choices and develop character, they need to belong, and they begin to anticipate the great transition from the nest-like security of school and home into the stormy challenge of the waiting world. I was passionate about teaching English, but the school focused so intensely on the program and test scores that it was difficult to diverge from coverage. I experimented with drama, group work, retreats, and excursions but was unsatisfied. Students were too often inert, isolated, and bored. Graduation was great theater, but seemed to be missing a great opportunity for educational meaning and lasting influence.

To search out responses to these and other issues about schooling that concerned me, I entered the doctoral program at Harvard to pursue studies and fieldwork in educational alternatives. My examination of individualized programs led me to write *Individualized Instruction: A Descriptive Analysis*, which demonstrated that most programs were only partially individualized for a few students for a short period of time. I was becoming interested in a fully developed alternative. That took shape when I met my new colleagues at Simon Fraser University and produced "Walkabout: Searching for the Right Passage from Childhood and School," which described a program for "challenging students to challenge themselves" and to earn their graduation by major projects in six areas: adventure, service, logical inquiry, creativity, careers, and practical applications. "Walkabout" became the most requested reprint in the history of the *Phi Delta Kappan*, Walkabout schools sprang up, and several have Internet Web pages on-line.

As a teacher of teachers at Simon Fraser, I specialized in the development of new educational programs. To model what I was teaching, I continued to explore the theory and practice of self-directed learning. I also shaped my courses around the principles of self-direction. Many students contributed to the development of the ideas and practices that became basic elements of my approach, especially those practicing teachers studying for their master's degrees at night. This did not happen without a struggle. After I outlined their first assignment to develop and implement a brief program based on their own ideas, there was a stir, and one student said indignantly, as if I had sinned against them, "What do you mean, our own ideas?" Since invention is the core of development, a long discussion followed as we all realized that thinking for oneself and acting on one's own ideas had been pushed aside in most classrooms by the pressure to cover content. That was the first of many concepts we developed together. The second was that students are wise and eager to become wiser.

During that time, I formed Challenge Education Associates with several colleagues to pursue the development of programs to teach self-directed learning and to provide teachers with our program, The Self-Directing Professional. Later, I founded Personal Power Press International, then wrote, published, and marketed several books about how to teach students to teach themselves. A group of us—teachers, parents, and professors—founded World Citizens for a Universal Curriculum and developed a world citizen passport that students earned by meeting a range of self-directed challenges in what we called the "Yes, I Can!" program. We thought it was promising but could not get it off the ground internationally. Sometimes the dragon wins.

This book is designed as a handbook for middle and high school teachers who want to help adolescents address the fundamental issues that they face. It is for teachers who want to empower students to manage their own learning. It is for those who want to prepare their students for the challenge of adulthood and to equip them with the tools and the passion for learning that will serve them throughout their lives.

Those who wish to pursue such a journey will find in the pages that follow an explanation of self-directed learning (SDL), a description of how to develop an SDL program, and a guide to the teaching techniques and tools required for helping students to become skilled in SDL. Such issues as assessment and motivation are dealt with fully, especially the motivation of exceptional and difficult students.

SDL is a challenge to teachers as well as students, but without challenge, there is little chance for reward. I hope that you will take this challenge and reap the wonderful rewards that the journey offers.

July 2002   Maurice Gibbons
Bowen Island, British Columbia

Acknowledgments

ALL OF US who create ideas and shape them into programs and then write papers and books stand on foundations built by those who have gone before us. We get our own work done only with the help of people around us who are guided by a vision similar to our own. My thanks especially to Stan Elam, former editor of the *Phi Delta Kappan*; adult educator Malcolm Knowles; and the late Bob Smith of Northern Illinois University for nurturing and contributing to new ideas about self-directed learning.

For years I worked so closely with a team of colleagues under the banner of Challenge Education Associates that some of the ideas in this book are as much theirs as mine. I am indebted to them for their partnership then and for their assistance with this book: Pat Holborn at Simon Fraser University; Peter Norman, educational consultant extraordinaire; and Gary Phillips, director of the National Schools Project based in Seattle. I am also indebted to my friend and colleague Milton McClaren: I asked for help, and he gave it. Thank you, also, to Matt Albee of Artmachine in Palo Alto for swift assistance in demanding times.

I thank the principals, teachers, and other officials at the schools featured in this book, especially those who permitted me to use their teaching materials as examples. They are Rita Hartman, principal of Orange Grove Middle School in Tucson, Arizona, and Joan Yates, director of the Waters Grant Project in Tucson; Ian Strachan, principal of Thomas Haney High School in Maple Ridge, British Columbia, and from the same school, English teacher Sandy Birce, math teachers Eric Proctor and Kuniko Nomura, and earth sciences teachers George McRae and Jeff Radom; Pat Sliemers and Jeff Bogard at Jefferson County Open School in Lakewood,

Colorado, along with its wonderful faculty; and Lennie Augustine, my teacher-contact at Saint Paul Open School. They gave me all of the assistance I asked for.

Ted and Nancy Sizer, through their assistant, Danielle Cambria, provided me with materials developed by the faculty at Francis W. Parker Charter Essential School in Devens, Massachusetts. I am also indebted to Brian Herrin, a science teacher from Sentinel High School in West Vancouver; Keith Butler, a social studies teacher at Oak Bay High School in Victoria; and math teachers Ray Faught, from Francis Kelsey Secondary School in Mill Bay, and Sue Baker, from Chemainus High School, and Rod MacVicar and Ruth Foster, science teachers at Centennial High School, all in British Columbia, Canada. I am deeply grateful for the open, generous assistance from all of these highly skilled educators, and I am proud to be associated with them. Although they permitted me to use their approaches to illustrate practices described in this book, that is not necessarily an indication that they subscribe to the positions and policies that I recommend.

I am also privileged to have the assistance of the founding administrators at three self-directed high schools: Wayne Jennings from St. Paul Open, Dave Estergaard from Thomas Haney, and Arnold Langberg from Jefferson County Open. They are pioneers who made important changes in traditional schooling, and made them last. Candice Spillsbury, a director in the Cowichan Valley School District in British Columbia, introduced me to Francis Kelsey Secondary School and reviewed the manuscript for this book.

I am indebted to my Jossey-Bass editor, Christie Hakim, for her patience, her whip, and her insistence on practicality. The editorial team that prepared the manuscript for publication—Carolyn Uno, Elizabeth Forsaith, and Beverly Miller—did an exceptional job. Thank you to them and to Rosemary Wall for her technical magic in preparing my drafts for submission. And I wish to say a much more than cursory thank you to my wife, Leslie, who took over the management of this manuscript and made it happen. I am deeply grateful for all of this extraordinary assistance. Any blemishes on the book that follows are mine.

M.G.

The Self-Directed Learning Handbook

Chapter 1

The Case for Self-Directed Learning

NOTHING is so natural to us as learning and accomplishment. We hunger for it from our first breath. We enter school already skilled in it and eager for more. We pursue it, often with passion, for the rest of our lives. The need to survive, become competent, find intimacy, and sustain self-esteem presses us forward on all life fronts. We search for a role and work of significance; for companionship, partner, and family; for understanding each other and ourselves; for mastery over something and for fulfillment. Our species is irrepressibly curious and restless; we question everything and seek answers; we see a need or possibility and press forward to see if we can make it real. The drive to learn can be suppressed—we can be deprived, beaten, and drugged—but these are only frictions to the unstoppable learning momentum that has propelled our species from its prehistoric beginnings to its current civilized state.

Self-directed learning (SDL) is designed to nurture this momentum, to broaden and deepen it, to help students channel and refine it. This design has been enhanced by a flood of recent discoveries about the brain. We have found that the brain is a meaning-making machine that thrives in rich environments, seeks out patterns, builds on previous experiences, and functions best in nonthreatening situations. Not only is the brain a dynamic, self-directing instrument of learning, it is highly individualized as well. Recent studies of intelligence, learning style, and talent or strengths affirm the great diversity in the ways people learn. Cognitive psychology has also focused on the importance of learning how to learn, that is, on developing the strategies that can be applied to any learning task. Such portable skills prepare any learner for the ultimate challenge of lifelong learning.

This attention to learning for life reminds us, as we address adolescent students in middle and high school, that we are dealing with a whole life—

not just intellect but emotions and performance as well. And it reminds us that adolescence is a life between childhood and adulthood. Major tasks in this chaotic teenage period include development in personality, character, and talent as well as in academics. The challenge of the transition is to leave childhood behind and to stand on the threshold of adulthood with purpose and confidence. This means maturing as a person, finding a social place, becoming independent, and finding a focus for work. The key to such readiness for students is self-efficacy, that feeling of certainty, forged in action, that they can set a course and then make the journey.

The journey into adulthood—into the world—has seldom been more challenging. Globalization is rapidly expanding the economic field of play. Change is dramatically shifting the nature of life and work. Knowledge is doubling every few years. Technology is transforming the way we live and the way we work. Work itself is transformed from the well-protected life-long job to the precarious short-term performance contract. Individuals will not be looked after from the cradle to the grave; increasingly, they must look after themselves. Students must know how to learn every day, how to adapt to rapidly shifting circumstances, and how to take independent initiative when opportunity disappears. SDL prepares students for this new world in which the active learner survives best.

What Is Self-Directed Learning?

SDL is any increase in knowledge, skill, accomplishment, or personal development that an individual selects and brings about by his or her own efforts using any method in any circumstances at any time. A student, for example, decides to build and launch rockets that will rise one mile into the atmosphere. He inspires others to join him. They go on the Internet, contact the National Aeronautics and Space Administration, consult with a science teacher, find a machine shop, build experimental models, and, after many attempts, succeed.

Teacher-directed learning (TDL) by contrast is any increase in a student's knowledge or skill brought about by initiatives taken by a teacher, which includes a selection of the learning to be accomplished, presentations about it, assigned study and practice activities, and a test to measure mastery. A teacher, for example, selects the topic of propulsion, presents lessons to all students showing the physics involved, assigns readings and questions about it in a textbook, conducts demonstrations with assembled rockets, and then tests students about their mastery of the principles.

Both are important approaches to learning. TDL is important because it is an efficient way to present new bodies of knowledge and practice. SDL is important because it enables students to customize their approach to learning tasks, combines the development of skill with the development of character, and prepares them for learning throughout their lives.

SDL is dramatically different from TDL. It requires a different approach by the teacher and demands new skills from students. In SDL, students gradually take over most of the teaching operations that are traditional in TDL until they are designing as well as executing their own learning activities. The teacher's role is transformed and becomes even more important and more demanding. Teaching SDL requires a full professional repertoire of instruction, including training, coaching, guiding, and counseling skills. It represents a paradigm shift in thinking about teaching and learning (see Table 1.1).

The choice, of course, is not simply between teacher-controlled and student-controlled learning. There are many stages between these two poles. Students can be taught to think for themselves, work at their own pace, learn in their own way, choose their own goals, and design their own programs. Each of these is a step toward SDL, and each can be the focus of a teacher's program. How far across this bridge any teacher decides to travel will be determined in part by individual judgment and the circumstances in which he or she works. This book is a challenge to teachers to challenge themselves to go as far as they can in this effort. Fortunately, as we will see, there are excellent schools to model each of these stages of SDL.

In TDL, we teach students about the nature of flight; in SDL, we teach students how to fly. When students learn to fly, they "earn their wings."

TABLE 1.1

Shifts in Thinking About Teaching and Learning

In teacher-directed learning, the teacher:	In student-directed learning, the teacher:
Decides the course goals and the content to be studied	Teaches students to set their own goals and eventually choose what they will study
Presents course content to students in lessons	Teaches students the skills and processes involved in setting goals, making plans, and initiating action
Sets exercises and assignments for study	Negotiates student proposals for learning and acting
Monitors completion and assesses accuracy of student work	Guides students through self-directed challenge activities
Tests and grades student performance	Reviews students' assessment of their work

They study in the classroom, work on simulations, and practice in the air with a flight instructor until they have the knowledge and skill to fly solo. When they prove that they can make skillful flights on their own, they can fly anywhere they choose. Teaching SDL is about teaching the skills and providing the experience that students need to guide their own learning lives. It is teaching them what they need in order to solo safely and successfully in life. SDL teachers, like flight instructors, succeed when their students no longer need them.

SDL not only encourages teachers to help students to find a passion; it requires it. In SDL, teachers not only challenge students to excel; they challenge students to challenge themselves to go as far as possible beyond the easy and familiar. SDL ends not in exercises but in action, and action as often as possible in the world beyond the classroom. Teachers do not direct students so much as they teach them to direct themselves by empowering them. SDL students work closely with other students and adults, not just independently. They are charged to learn academics, but are challenged with much more as well.

This approach equips the teacher with the means to inspire a wide range of students to learn. The program, as we will see in Chapter Seven, is designed around motivational principles: it cultivates students' interests, applies their strengths, and equips them for success. Such features enable the teacher to adapt the program to every student. The teacher is each student's partner in becoming proficient. Mark, for instance, was a problem student who had moved to several other schools before he entered an SDL program. As he put it,

> I'm just grateful to be here. I was going nowhere at my other schools. Look at me! I'm too big to be bossed around like a little kid. Then I get here and they treat you with respect. I get a part in a little theater thing about Galileo at the museum, talk to the lab guys there, and here I am doing a science project on solar emissions.

The teacher's task is to help students like Mark to find their passion and then to challenge them to pursue it. Eileen was not aggressive but passive, so passive it became resistance:

> I can't believe it. I had teachers lecturing me all the time to get to work. Then I get into this classroom, and she tells me to challenge myself. Now she's got me telling myself to do stuff I don't even think I can do.

In SDL all students can find a pathway to progress and receive recognition for it.

For bright and talented students, such programs often provide an opportunity to run free, move fast, and go far. Meguido, a student in a challenging SDL program, viewed coming to this class as a relief: "No more dragging along as slow as the slowest guy. You can just go for it." SDL also offers equal opportunity for students who, in regular TDL situations, have always been ranked against the brightest and considered relative failures. Such ranking and its diminishing message are deadly educational medicine.

Every SDL teacher is committed to the success of all students—to the discovery and development of strengths and to measuring personal progress, not rank. Such features enable teachers to engage both students who are proficient and students who are struggling. Tough, streetwise Jeremy finds success learning to fly an airplane. Bottom-of-the-class dweller Maria discovers that she can draw. While developing these interests and gaining recognition for their success, such students learn that they can accomplish, and as a result, their other efforts also improve.

SDL teachers enjoy a number of advantages when working with students of all kinds. As students learn how to learn, or how to teach themselves, they often work individually and independently. This enables the teacher to meet with individuals and small groups regularly for the special attention and guidance that are so important to this process. But teaching SDL is demanding. It means teaching students all they need to know in order to learn a course on their own and devise their own studies. Fortunately, every teacher is already using several SDL approaches (see Resource A at the end of this book) that provide a solid foundation on which to build a full program.

In the future, technology will replace teachers whose major role is to present content. That is already happening as a result of open learning institutes, cyberschools, and on-line high school courses. As Gary Phillips, director of the National School Improvement Project, says, "Anyone who can be replaced by a computer should be" (personal communication to the author). The teacher who teaches students how to learn, guides them through the struggles of adolescence, and challenges them to challenge themselves to excel will always be irreplaceable. The secret of SDL is education that goes deeper. As one teacher said whose students have to complete a series of SDL challenge projects, known as passages, to graduate, "I like the adventure passage best because the journey leads students to the adventure of self-discovery, and that is the greatest discovery of all." Students can direct their learning only when they begin to know themselves and the direction they want their lives to take.

The rewards for SDL teachers are great. Not the least of the pleasures is to hear students presenting at the end of their program describe the drama of taking charge of their own learning. Their pride in prevailing during their struggles to accomplish their goals can be overwhelming. Once teachers are touched, the experience becomes a necessity. As this teacher from Jefferson County Open School in Lakewood, Colorado, said,

> *We want our kids to identify their passion and to pursue it with discipline. Once they care, they can't be stopped, and they can recreate what they accomplish again and again, growing stronger every time. That's why I can't pour information into empty tubes again. Once you've been close to the fire, you can't live without it any more.*

How Does Research Support SDL?

Recent research on teaching is usually interpreted as guidelines for improving how to teach students the curriculum. Teachers are urged to apply the research on learning styles, for example, by designing their lessons to accommodate the different ways—visual, auditory, tactile, and kinesthetic—by which students most readily comprehend and apply what they are taught. When brain research shows that people learn better when new concepts are tied to what students already know, teachers are encouraged to connect the lesson to students' past experience and to begin with their current state of knowledge about the subjects they are teaching. Such responses are commendable and promising for TDL. With a shift in perspective, however, we can also see, in these and many other findings, the outline of another paradigm in which students exercise their individual learning styles in creating their own meaning. That paradigm is SDL. We can flesh out that paradigm with other research and the developments based on it.

The work on multiple intelligences, diverse learning styles, and the psychology of the individual is applied in various approaches to teaching designed to accommodate those differences in direct instruction. This involves teaching to the intelligences and learning styles and individualizing instruction. From another point of view, however, we can affirm that each child is unique, with a unique set of talents, a unique body of experience, and a unique perspective on the world. Students learn best in unique ways that maximize their personal resources. It seems reasonable to conclude that students will learn best by coherently extending their experience in their own emerging style that takes full advantage of their individual strengths.

The basic concept of metacognition is that we think about our thoughts: we think about what we know, what we are doing, and what we are thinking. As Hacker, Dunlosky, and Graesser (1998) say, the promise of metacognitive theory is that it focuses "on those characteristics of thinking that can contribute to students' awareness and understanding of being self-regulatory organisms, that is of being agents of their own thinking" (p. 20). One of the ways this theory has been applied is to teach students to self-regulate their learning and study practices in TDL classrooms (Zimmerman, Bonner, and Kovach, 1996). From another perspective, metacognition is the key to SDL. Students learn to think for themselves, make plans, and take action. They think about their thoughts in order to make good decisions and about their decisions to ensure successful action. They think about the process they will follow, solutions to problems that arise, and ways to improve their performance. SDL is built on metacognitive competencies.

The application of neurological research in brain-compatible teaching emphasizes that the brain seeks patterns and meaning, requires stimulating experiences and environments, learns best with active involvement in the activity at hand and active involvement with others, and responds poorly under threat. These are often translated into better TDL practices that seem to work well to enhance learning (Neve, Hart, and Thomas, 1988). Teachers can trace out patterns in history, the sciences, and the arts, but how much more powerful it is to teach students to find the patterns themselves, and then to analyze the patterns they discover and draw conclusions from them. In SDL, learning leads to action and involves students in both helping each other and working together to learn. Teachers seek the success of all students without threatening competition that generates many losers. SDL is very brain compatible.

Developmental psychology reminds us that there is another curriculum of fundamental interest to the student but not a high priority in most TDL school programs: the curriculum of personal growth and maturation, that is, the curriculum of personal transformation and transition. In this psychosocial curriculum that students cannot avoid, the central task is to establish a healthy personality and unique identity, that is, a coherent sense of oneself that others confirm (Erikson, 1959). This sense of self is nurtured by accomplishment and acknowledged competence. At the same time, adolescents are making the transition from childhood toward adulthood, which requires them to become more independent, responsible, competent, and hopeful. Making these transformations and transitions is a challenging task, and a successful outcome is not guaranteed. Success requires the development of values and character. Educational programs, including courses, should be compatible with and contribute to students' successful achievement of this transformation and transition. SDL activities, especially challenges and passages—extended projects often conducted in the field—are designed to guide and support students through their struggles to complete the tasks of personal transformation and to equip them for the rigors of the transition from childhood to young adulthood.

Constructivist theory (Kelly, 1955) claims that building meaning is our basic role and that we should build meaning by conducting scientific-like investigations regularly to gather evidence on which to base the concepts we hold. We should do more than construct meaning; we should also reconstruct concepts and theories that are no longer satisfactory. We can teach students the ideas we want them to adopt, or we can teach them to create meaning for themselves. Philip Candy, in his excellent book on SDL (1991), concludes that teaching students to make their own meaning is the main task of self-directed learning. Teaching students to think for themselves, to think systematically, to draw their own conclusions, and to construct their own perspective on their lives and the world are the basic purposes of SDL.

Marilee Sprenger (1999, p. 14) concludes that "humans are social creatures and learning is a social activity." But how valuable is group work as a method of learning? Johnson and Johnson (1991) answer the question succinctly:

> *There is a great deal of research indicating that, if student-student interdependence is structured carefully and appropriately, students will achieve at a higher level, use higher level reasoning strategies more frequently, have higher levels of achievement motivation, be more intrinsically motivated, develop more positive interpersonal relationships with each other, value the subject area being studied more, have higher self-esteem, and be more skilled interpersonally. [p. 17]*

But, as Johnson and Johnson (1991) warn, these benefits cannot be enjoyed by simply grouping students. The essentials of cooperative learning must be in place. Teachers have to teach students positive interdependence, face-to-face promotive interaction, individual accountability, cooperative skill, and group processing. These are essential guidelines for both teachers and students of SDL. Life is a social activity, successful action often involves teamwork and social savvy, individuals need interaction to learn about themselves, and group work is often the doorway to success in SDL. As Lev Vygotsky said, "What students can do together today they can do alone tomorrow" (Johnson and Johnson, 1991, p. 57).

William James once wrote, "If you care enough about a result you will almost certainly attain it." In his thorough book *Motivating Humans* (1992), Martin E. Ford states that in terms of motivation, "research shows that little else matters if there is no relevant goal in place" (p. 220). The potency of the goal to inspire behavior is influenced by personal agency beliefs, which encompass capability beliefs (Can I do it?), context beliefs (Will this activity be supported by a responsive environment?) and the strength and nature of the emotions related to the goal. Ford states that "goals lose their potency in the absence of clear and informative feedback" (p. 220). And he advises that challenging but attainable goals are motivating, especially when they are associated with several desirable outcomes. Flexible standards and rules protect people from demotivation and encourage them to undertake improvements. These simple principles from his motivational system make an excellent outline of the principles of SDL and offer a pattern of practices that can be taught to students as a guide to motivating themselves.

Robert Sternberg in *Successful Intelligence* (1997) describes characteristics of successful people based on his research into analytical, creative, and practical intelligence. The characteristics are also major themes of SDL. Successfully intelligent people, he says, generate good ideas and translate them into action, think in terms of processes leading to productivity, and motivate themselves to action. Successfully intelligent people are highly self-directed.

When we examine these examples of trends in research from another perspective, we see in them not confirmation of traditional TDL, but the structural beams of another paradigm, and that paradigm is SDL.

The Major Principles of an SDL Program

SDL programs rest on five principles:

1. *Programs should be congruent with a life of learning, the natural ways we learn, and the unique methods by which each of us learns best.* The basic assumption of SDL is that from birth to death, we live lives of learning: we first learn to function, then to live well, and finally to make a difference. Learning is a natural process outlined by both the history of our species and our history as individuals. Our success depends on the range, depth, and quality of the learning we achieve. Each of us exhibits and develops these natural capacities in an individual way according to the talents we are endowed with, the experiences we encounter, the strengths we discover, the interests that begin to direct and motivate us, and the patterns of

learning that we develop. An SDL program should be congruent with these lifelong, natural, and individual learning drives.

2. *Programs should be adapted to the maturation, transformations, and transitions that adolescent students experience.* Adolescents experience rapid physical, cerebral, and hormonal change that is often destabilizing. Among the transformations or passages that they must address, the most important is establishing and confirming a personal, stable identity. Key features of this formation are the development of reflection, character, and competence. The major transition they face is from dependent childhood to independent early adulthood in which they must secure new freedoms and meet the responsibilities that go with them. SDL programs are designed to cultivate the successful accomplishment of these changes in the pursuit of excellence as a person.

3. *Programs should be concerned with all aspects of a full life.* Academic studies are important and included in an SDL program, but so also are the personal, social, and technical domains of human experience. The personal domain focuses on the cultivation of the individual's talents, values, and interests. The social domain is concerned with the individual's ability to relate to others, to learn from them, and to work with them. In the technical domain, emphasis is placed on competence, performance, and productivity. In SDL, focus on these domains is as important as focus on academics, in part for their contribution to academic success but in the main because they are the foundation for a successful life of learning.

4. *Learning in SDL programs should employ a full range of human capacities, including our senses, emotions, and actions as well as our intellects.* SDL is grounded in direct experience. Experience is absorbed by finely honed senses. The mind reflects, investigates, and plans. Feelings stir, drive, and direct our thoughts and efforts. But our senses, feelings, and thoughts all focus on action, the application to productivity, and the production of palpable outcomes. SDL is designed to hone awareness, cultivate drive, encourage thoughtful conclusions, and shape plans that all lead to the successful achievement of challenging results.

5. *SDL activities should be conducted in settings suited to their development.* The classroom is a useful setting if it is converted to serve SDL, but even converted it is a limited environment. Many experiences can be brought into the classroom directly or indirectly through simulation, computers, and other media. But SDL thrives best when the setting is expanded to include a broader range of people to learn from and places in which to learn. This begins with the local community and spreads outward to include the widest possible experience of challenge in the world. Many

studies are learned best on site. We learn about others and their lives by knowing them directly and working with them. We develop character by service and other caring acts. We learn by challenging ourselves in real-world situations.

The Essential Elements of SDL

Any SDL activity, course, or program based on these five fundamental principles will also feature these essential elements:

• *Student control over as much of the learning experience as possible.* The major shift from TDL to SDL is a shift in the locus of control from the teacher to the student. For the student, this represents a shift from outer control to inner control, which reflects the major change under way in the lives of adolescents as they begin to establish themselves as individuals separate from their childhood dependencies. During these years, they begin to shape their own opinions and ideas, make their own decisions, choose their own activities, take more responsibility for themselves, and enter the world of work. Charging students with the task of developing their own learning turns them to their own resources, which develops their emerging individuality and helps them to rehearse more adult roles. As they become more self-directing, they not only learn effectively but become more themselves.

• *Skill development.* Inner control is aimless unless students learn to focus and apply their talents and energies intensely. For this reason, the emphasis in SDL is on the development of skills and processes that lead to productive activity. Students learn to achieve course outcomes, think independently, and plan and execute their own activities. These processes, and the skills involved in them, come together in student proposals for study and action. Students prepare and then negotiate them with their teachers, often in the form of written agreements that become records of the contracts that they negotiate. The intent is to provide a framework that enables students to identify their interests and equips them to realize them successfully.

• *Students' learning to challenge themselves to their best possible performance.* Self-direction is dormant without challenge. First, teachers challenge students, and then they challenge these students to challenge themselves. Challenge requires reaching for a new level of performance in a familiar field or launching an adventure into a new field of interest. It means setting the standard of achievement a step higher than one can readily achieve. Challenging oneself means taking the risk to go beyond the easy and familiar. For those willing, it means reaching regularly for performances that demand from them the very best they have to offer. The challenge is to go out far and in deep. It is the challenge of the journey heroes take when they leave their safe and familiar surroundings to undertake a task of great significance. In the struggle that ensues, they attain an insight and power that changes their lives and enables them to return and contribute to the communities from which their journeys began.

• *Student self-management—that is, management of themselves and their learning enterprises.* In SDL, choices and freedoms are matched by self-control and responsibilities. Students learn to express self-control by searching for, and making a commitment to, core personal interests and aspirations. In this process, they determine not only what they will do but the kind of performer they will become. SDL requires confidence, courage, and determination to energize the effort involved. Students develop these attributes as they become skilled in managing their own time and effort and the resources they need to conduct their work. Even well-organized efforts run aground. In the face of obstacles, students learn to face their difficulties, find alternatives, and solve their problems in order to maintain effective productivity. The combination of inner resources and performative skill required for self-management in SDL is the same process students will require for the successful management of growth and productivity throughout their lives.

• *Self-motivation and self-assessment.* Many principles of motivation are built into the design of SDL, such as the pursuit of one's own high-interest goals. When students adopt these principles, they become the major elements of self-motivation. By setting important goals for themselves, arranging for feedback on their work, and achieving success, they learn to inspire their own efforts. Similarly, students learn to evaluate their own progress: they assess both the quality of their work and the process that they designed to conduct it. In SDL, assessment is an essential means of learning and learning how to learn: improvement flows from students' critical assessment of their own activities. Students often initiate self-evaluation in the learning agreements that they submit to teachers by including a description of the standards they will strive to attain. Since the responsibility for proving that they have achieved their goals lies with the students, they gather their proofs and products in a portfolio, which becomes the focus of the evaluation. Just as self-motivation energizes students to produce the achievements that are evaluated, self-assessment motivates students to seek the best achievement possible.

These five elements outline the underlying structure of SDL activities and programs. They also describe the challenge of SDL for the teacher as well as for the student. Many programs permit self-direction; too few teach students how to be self-directed. The focus in what follows is on teaching SDL.

Approaching SDL in Stages

Teachers leaning toward an SDL approach often ask, "Do I have to plunge right in and teach a full-blown self-directed program?" For teachers steeped in the TDL tradition, the switch can be intimidating. Fortunately, there are a number of alternative approaches to choose from. The four we will be emphasizing in the pages ahead are teaching students to think independently, teaching students to manage their own learning, teaching students to plan their own learning, and teaching students to direct their own learning. Each of these alternatives can be regarded as a stage in the transition to SDL, a transition that enables both teachers and students to master their new roles in teaching and learning gradually. The second question teachers ask is, "How do I go about introducing SDL into my classroom?" To answer this question, we have developed a five-step process that involves identifying the outcomes of the course you are teaching, creating an environment that supports SDL activities, teaching the skills and processes that students need to direct their own learning, negotiating with students the proposals that they present for learning, and setting in place a procedure for student self-assessment. The following chapter describes this process.

• • •

There are many pathways to SDL, but all lead students to the skillful and passionate pursuit of their own learning. This can be accomplished only by dedicated teachers who are committed to this vision and equipped to empower their students to become fully and proudly themselves.

Chapter 2

A Framework for Teaching SDL

WHAT MUST TEACHERS DO to develop an SDL program? There are many ways to answer this question; there are always different ways to develop a program. This chapter cuts through the possibilities and presents a basic approach that is practical and workable in any classroom where any subject is taught. The approach that follows is based on practices that have been tested in many classrooms and can be applied in some form by any teacher who has decided to introduce his or her students to some form of self-directed learning.

Teachers who are beginning to move from TDL to SDL will be undertaking as many new skills as their students will. They can approach the change in a number of ways that range from sampling SDL teaching ideas to developing a complete SDL program. Teachers can teach students to think independently about course issues, to work through course study materials on their own, to plan their own approaches to achieving course expectations, or to design and pursue their own learning plans. By introducing these four approaches in sequence, teachers gradually increase the degree of self-direction required. Bridging the gap between TDL and SDL in this way offers both teachers and their students the opportunity to accumulate systematically the skills and experiences they need to be successful.

Whatever approach to self-direction teachers choose, they will benefit from a framework for developing a complete program. The following five elements are basic and, followed in sequence, they may be regarded as steps in the process of SDL development.

- Identify the course outcomes that students must achieve to complete the course or program.

- Create an environment suitable for enacting course outcomes.

- Teach students the skills and practices necessary for achieving course outcomes.

- Negotiate with each student the proposal, contract, or plan she or he has prepared for achieving both course and personal outcomes.

- Set in place a process for student self-assessment and a procedure for monitoring their progress.

Defining the Course

Defining your course so that students and others can see what has to be done to complete it is accomplished by translating the subject matter of the course into outcomes that the student must achieve. These outcomes are expressed in statements like this: "The student will be able to explain the process of photosynthesis." There is no ideal number of outcomes, but fifteen to twenty-five for a single course seems to be a good range that balances thoroughness of coverage with manageability for students.

When the content is converted to outcomes, many different approaches become possible. Rather than steer students through the textbook and worksheets to cover the headings in the curriculum guide and to prepare them for the test, the teacher sees the task and is challenged to ask, "What is the most compelling, efficient, and elegant way to achieve that outcome?" Once the fix on the textbook is broken, a full range of presentations, experiences, and activities is opened.

Outcomes also make the course accessible to students. Often the teacher is the only one who knows what students must learn in order to complete the course. Some teachers guard that knowledge carefully to maintain tight control over the program, and the course always continues to the end of the term allotted for it. In contrast, once the course outcomes are defined, the teacher can challenge students to achieve them in their own ways. The challenge can take a variety of forms. It can, for example, be converted into a question ("What is the process of photosynthesis?") that can be answered by a class investigation, in small group activities, or through individual projects.

Outcomes also enable the teacher to plan a variety of SDL activities. They can provide the focus for a series of learning guides or packages, which outline the tasks that students must complete to attain each outcome, the resources available, and the proof of attainment required. Students can then pursue these guides at their own pace and often in their own ways. Students can also take course outcomes and devise their own approaches to achieving them in groups or individually. Outcomes, expressed as challenges, offer frameworks within which students can devise their own goals and plans. A challenge to conduct a logical inquiry, for example, enables each student to choose a different issue to investigate and to develop a personal strategy for completing the task.

By defining course outcomes, we make SDL possible. Defining the course enables students to set and pursue their own learning enterprises.

Expanding Learning Options and Environments

When students begin to pursue course outcomes or their own outcomes individually, they require a new classroom support system that is appropriate for their new learning activities, one that offers more learning options, more freedom of movement, a suitable environment, and new rules of order. Expanding course options means increasing the number and range of choices for learning available to students. With that increase in learning options, we also include providing the appropriate environment for self-directed work, one with a climate that enhances rather than impedes individual pursuits. Each time we increase the degree of SDL, the demand for options increases.

A switch to SDL shifts the entire process of teaching and learning. The structures that were designed for teacher direction are not suitable for student self-direction. A class in which each student is pursuing a different program, using different resources, and often conferring with others will not function smoothly in a traditional classroom, with traditional resources, traditional order, and a climate of control and competition. Increasing the learning options for students requires more teacher preparation, but it also creates time and opportunity; while students work independently, the teacher has the opportunity to provide many new forms of instruction and guidance that can significantly improve student performance.

All of the approaches to SDL require the development of new instructional materials. The more choices that the approach offers, the more options must be provided to support student choices. As students begin to operate independently, the way the class functions has to change as well so that students can move freely, consult with each other, and work in groups. This new pattern requires a classroom designed to accommodate it and the addition of as many other locations as can be arranged. Such freedom of movement and the exercise of new responsibilities in a more open environment can be successful only under a new order in which students accept responsibility for self-control and self-management. Such responsibilities flourish best in an atmosphere that combines personal safety, mutual respect, and industry with an expectation of success. Taken together, these changes describe a learning community in which students become teachers and teachers become students, all working together in the learning enterprise.

Whether students are learning from the teacher as a class, from packages, in groups, or individually, the lessons or units usually involve experience, study, and productive activity, the three primary SDL methods. Here are a few of the kinds of options often presented or made available to students:

Classes

- Presentations introducing the subject or discipline, its structure, the modes of inquiry employed, the questions or issues it deals with, and the major concepts on which it is based

- Shared investigations, inquiries, and problems to solve

- Debates, trials, case studies, and dramatizations

- Training in SDL skills and processes using demonstrations, rehearsal, guided practices, and group or individual application

Groups

- Training in group work skills: participating, organizing, communication, problem solving, and conflict resolution

- Planning and achieving course outcomes as a group

- Designing and conducting the group's own units and projects

Individual

- Training in skills and processes for learning individually: goal setting, planning, and evaluating

- Learning to manage themselves: developing the perspective, attitudes, and initiative that make SDL possible

- Thinking independently: learning to analyze, conclude, argue, and create

- Managing time and effort to complete learning packages for achieving course outcomes

- Designing and completing their own plans for achieving course outcomes

- Designing and completing activities to achieve their own outcomes

Presenting such activities requires a range of teaching skills and the preparation of new teaching-learning materials. They also involve arranging for a rich array of learning resources such as reference books, computers, and VCRs. Learning options can also be increased by expanding the range of sites available to students for learning.

Teachers should begin by bringing into the classroom as much as they can of what they need from available school resources, and then they should enable students to use the resources available in the school for learning—for example, the library, the computer room, a theater stage, a video room, or shops of various kinds. Next, they can access anything in the community that can be reached and used in a day—libraries, museums, theaters, universities, houses of worship, hospitals, businesses, industries, and natural environments. These options include resources for study, experiences, and work, and they put students in contact with people who can be teachers and mentors. Sites outside the community offer experiences so dramatic that they are worth the enormous effort required: a visit to New York City or a farm, to the site of an earthquake or an archaeological dig, or to Mexico or London can be powerful and unforgettable experiences that open students' minds about themselves, others, and the world. The goal is to make everywhere a classroom and learning unforgettable. These are not far-fetched options: with a year to plan, fundraisers, and supereconomical travel, such amazing experiences are available to many.

Finally, we increase the options open to students by creating an environment that encourages them to be actively self-directing and makes that possible. The encouragement comes from a positive, cooperative, nonthreatening climate in which the students feel that they can take a risk with support and that they can dare to dream. Using the options means being able to move easily from class meetings to small group work to individual activities. It means access to the technological equipment and other resources, access to the teacher, and access to resources beyond the classroom. It means the right to move freely and to interact with others, as well as the right to privacy and quiet for reflective work.

To make these options possible, students must learn to balance their new freedoms and opportunities with the exercise of responsibility and self-control. One way is to begin by establishing a code of conduct at the beginning of the course. This is done best in a teacher-led discussion to generate guidelines that are clear to everyone, endorsed by everyone, and then listed on a chart. These guidelines may be revised later, and the issue of self-control may have to be revisited often. The best guide to self-control is high motivation and compelling work. (Chapter Seven addresses motivation.)

Building Independent Thinking Skills

Students of SDL have a great deal to learn. In any subject, they have to meet the requirements of the course and learn how to do it independently. In addition, they have to learn how to set their own goals and achieve them. To accomplish these tasks, students must also learn a great deal about themselves and working with others, as well as how to study and take action. All of these activities require the exercise of skills and processes.

The key skill clusters are concerned with thinking independently and taking action. In TDL, students are often told what to know and are questioned until they can repeat the one acceptable right answer. Searching for right answers may explain why, in *The Disciplined Mind* (1999), Howard Gardner concluded from "a vast body of research" that "even the best students in our best schools do not understand very much of the curricular content" (p. 120). In SDL, memorizing information for recall on tests does not play a central role unless circumstances demand it. Knowing how to think for oneself does. It is the first step toward self-direction. Independent action begins with independent thinking.

The most important process of thinking autonomously is investigation—the method by which individuals make meaning for themselves. Investigation begins with a question to answer. The question is followed by the development of a strategy for finding evidence that will lead to a defensible conclusion. If the conclusion is questionable, the student may then devise a test to determine its validity. Through such investigations, students gather data, develop concepts, formulate opinions, mount arguments, and raise further questions. From the concepts they develop, they build a perspective on the world.

In SDL, learning is never static. As in the rest of life, it is usually moving toward action. The action process comprises related skills that students must learn in order to function successfully: goal setting, planning, self-management, problem solving, and self-assessment. Thinking independently prepares students to decide what to learn and accomplish, but in formulating their own activities, they must turn inward to discover their strengths and interests. With a goal that matters, students are ready to devise a plan of strategies in sequence to achieve it efficiently. Once the plan is in place, they can consider how to manage it successfully: how to schedule time, gather resources, and remain motivated to the end. When students launch their learning plans, they record their activities, especially the problems they face, solutions they devise, and the modifications in their plans that result. Finally, they devise a means of assessment that enables them to monitor their progress and demonstrate to others the level of success that they have achieved. Learning the skills of thinking independently and taking productive action equip students for SDL and for learning throughout their lives.

Negotiating Student Learning Agreements

The student learning agreement, or contract, is the students' own learning guide. In self-managed learning, they work through the teacher's learning guides. In self-planned and self-directed learning, they design and follow their own guides. The contract is a special form of proposal that outlines the planning process and becomes a guide to the student for thinking through the learning activity. Typically, it is a design for action that requires students to set their goals and explain them, plan their activities, prepare their resources, schedule their time, and devise a strategy for self-assessment. Completing a contract prepares students to apply the skills of productive action.

Once students have completed their proposals, they are ready to present them to the teacher. The contract is an excellent instrument for the student-teacher conference because it expresses clearly and concisely what the student is proposing and why. Students usually prepare for the conference by developing their ideas and vetting their learning proposals in support groups composed of two or three peers and in their larger advisory groups—each of which is about a half or third of the class—led by the teacher. When their plans are ready, students negotiate the terms with the teacher. Contracts enable teachers to see quickly what their students intend and to discuss each element of their proposal with them. Negotiation is a delicate process in which the teacher must guide students to success while maintaining their interest in the activity and their confidence that they can be successful.

Meeting with the teacher one-on-one is a highly motivating experience and the first challenge that students face in the pursuit of their projects. Determining one's own learning is an exciting and intimidating prospect, and discussing it with teachers to secure their agreement and support is a challenging initiative. It is also a valuable learning experience in which a proposal's strengths can be identified, new possibilities can be added, and potential problems can be identified and addressed.

Once negotiated, agreed on, and signed by both parties (a parent may be included too), the contract serves as a record of the agreement and a guide to teachers as they monitor the student's progress. It also serves both parties as a guide to assessment. Since students devise their own assessment plans, they have a means of ongoing feedback about their performance, and the teacher has a framework for monitoring it. Plans are often renegotiated after students actually experience what they conceived. The contract is an excellent record on which to base that process. With an agreed-on plan and a standard for demonstrating achievement, evaluation through self-assessment can be readily accomplished. If external assessment is advised or required, it can be added to the contract.

When the contract is complete, the teacher can add comments, and the student can file it in a personal portfolio of the year's or term's work.

The contract thus serves as a mini-curriculum that requires students to think through their proposed activities and to prepare for them carefully. It enables teachers to teach and to guide students through the action learning process, and it provides both a basis for assessment and a permanent record of accomplishment.

Establishing Assessment Processes

Circumstances often compel teachers to test, rank, and grade students, but in SDL, students learn to assess themselves and report on their own achievement because it is an essential part of the self-directing process. Students learn to assess their goals, plans, and procedures as well as their results or products, and they learn to assess themselves as learners. These critical reviews guide students to improvements that require attention and help them to identify strengths they can build on. They report their assessment and provide reasons or proof to support it. A framework of assessment strategies equips students and enables teachers to monitor and assist them.

When students submit a contract, it can contain an assessment section in which they propose how their achievements will be measured. One way is to establish a baseline performance and then describe what a satisfactory and an excellent improvement will be. Another is to describe criteria that can be applied to the finished product or performance.

In competencies that everyone must accomplish, such as learning to write compositions, rubrics can be supplied. A rubric is a model of performance at a particular level of proficiency. The composition rubric, for example, may have typical examples of five levels of performance, from beginner to expert, with descriptions of the features that must be exhibited to achieve that level. This is an excellent example of self-assessment that serves learning. Students know where they are and what they must do to be successful.

The third approach is through the portfolio, which may include the student's working journal and a transcript. The portfolio is a collection of proofs of achievement, products or representations of them, and possibly test scores from other activities. The portfolio in English might include, for example, an original short story, photographs of costumes designed for a play, and a test taken on the novel. The journal is a working journal—that is, the students' own record of ideas, plans, and struggles with implementation that may be included in the portfolio if the student chooses. A transcript is a more for-mal description by students of what they attempted, achieved, and learned in the course or program. The portfolio is the evidence students present that the outcomes they were given have been achieved.

A fourth approach is through student-centered conferencing, which includes both the negotiation of contracts with the teacher and the student's presentation of what he or she has learned to parents and other interested adults at report time. This introduces assessment through demonstration and presentation. Presentation to others is a powerful motivator and focus for effort. Students stand before an audience and present what they aspired to and what they achieved. Through exhibits, testimonials, and perfor-mances, they prove their accomplishments. Making such presentations is a challenge in itself, and it is the grounds for celebration of all that has been accomplished, including the demonstration itself. (Assessment is explained more fully in Chapter 8.)

• • •

These are the basic steps in the SDL approach to coursework: prepare a set of outcomes that encapsulates the course, expand the options for learning, teach the skills and processes that students need, negotiate their learning propos-als with them and launch them into their projects, monitor their progress, and review with them their assessments of what they have achieved.

Chapter 3

Rethinking Student Coursework

IN TRADITIONAL CLASSROOMS, teachers assume that they will set the goals for a course, plan a series of lessons through which to present the course content, organize exercises for students to practice what they learned, and then prepare a few tests and an exam to generate grades. As we go through the stages toward SDL, each of these teacher-directed structures is eliminated, until in pure SDL, they are all gone, along with the infrastructure to support them. Now we have to rethink the structure of learning and the supporting infrastructure of the classroom so that both are devoted to the complete success of self-directed students and the SDL program they are taking. Rethinking coursework means thinking about how to teach students to design their own learning and then deciding what kind of support system will enable their success.

Essential Planning Steps

Teaching students personal program design begins with teaching them to do what teachers up to this time have done for them. They must learn how to set their own goals or outcomes, plan their own action learning sequences, organize themselves and the resources they need, complete the work, and determine the level of success they achieved. Each of these elements is a skill that students need to be taught, and the whole is a process of interrelated skills that equips them to learn anything, anywhere, and at any time in their lives.

The SDL course changes as dramatically for the teacher as it does for the student. The gradual transformation from TDL to SDL parallels the transforming experience of students.

1. State the outcomes that students must achieve in order to complete the course (for example, "Students will understand the dynamics of the solar system").

2. Decide on an approach that will enable students to achieve the course outcomes (for example, prepare learning guides that students can study to understand the solar system, or set up teams to design their own units for studying the solar system).

3. Provide the materials and infrastructure necessary for the SDL approach to work successfully (for example, prepare learning guides, offer training in group work, and provide such resources as computers, telescope access, astronomer contact, and night sky experience).

4. Prepare the teaching roles that will be required to guide students to the successful achievement of the outcomes—either the outcomes assigned or the outcomes that students propose for themselves.

Understanding the Stages of SDL

The central decision for teachers moving toward SDL is determining how they will present the course. The question is, "How will we, as a class, operate to achieve self-direction?" The answer is to select one of the four stages or approaches to SDL: teaching students to think independently, teaching self-managed learning, teaching self-planned learning, or teaching self-directed learning. Each stage is a unique approach, and each stage in the sequence transfers more responsibility for course planning to the student. As a result, each stage requires a different kind of course preparation by the teacher and a different kind of infrastructure. Here is a brief introduction to the requirements for each stage.

Students Thinking Independently

In this stage, the classroom operates in a familiar TDL way, with the teacher instructing and directing student activities, but the nature and intent of the activities are very different. The challenge of this approach is to lead students from dependence on the teacher's thinking to dependence on their own thinking. The teacher shifts from recitation to provocation, from telling to asking, and from instruction to guidance, teaching students to think and find out for themselves. In this approach, course outcomes become questions to be investigated, thought through, and debated. For example, an outcome that states, "Students will understand mechanical advantage" becomes simply, "What is mechanical advantage, and how is it achieved?" The teacher introduces the questions, problems, and issues that comprise the course and orchestrates the investigations through which students pursue their answers. Sometimes these investigations are conducted as a class, and sometimes they are pursued in small groups or through individual activities. Students learn to analyze the situation, gather evidence, formulate their arguments, present their positions, and defend the conclusions they reach. In the arts, where the focus is on critical appreciation and the development of personal values, students learn to express their own judgment and opinion about the works that they study, but the emphasis on evidence and argument remains paramount.

Answering the questions that focus on the outcomes of the course is important, but even more important is the students' mastery of the processes by which they develop convincing answers. For this reason, the second emphasis is on investigative skills and processes. Students learn to think about and plan the best possible way to derive and confirm the answers they are seeking. The third level of thinking independently is students thinking about their own questions, interests, and ideas.

Teaching Self-Managed Learning

In self-managed learning, the teacher converts the course to learning packages that students can work their way through at their own pace. The learning package can take many forms, but all of them tell students what is to be learned, how they should go about learning it, and what they have to do to prove they have completed one package and are ready to go on to the next. A package may simply say, "Read the following pages . . . Complete the following questions . . . Request the answer key from your teacher." The challenge for teachers is to go as far as possible beyond this raw framework by matching each outcome with the most effective learning experiences possible. Packages can use the media, connect students to special instructional opportunities, and steer them to community sites. With the packages ready, the teacher can then devise a program to teach students the skills that they need to complete them: setting goals, scheduling time, and organizing their learning efforts.

Each package should include a means of assessment, which may be self-administered or teacher directed as long as progress is monitored regularly. The learning is provided; the key aspect of SDL involved is the students' ability to manage their learning activities effectively on their own.

Students working at their own pace will finish at different times; some will finish very quickly, and others will struggle to finish in the time allotted for the course. Both teachers and students benefit when exciting new possibilities await those who finish. These may include choices among special activities outside the course curriculum. One choice may be for students to create personal packages in pursuit of their own learning adventures. The course may be devised so that the basics are covered in packages that can be completed by most students in two-thirds of the course time, leaving one-third for activities that the students devise for themselves.

Self-Planned Learning

In self-planned learning, students decide for themselves how they will achieve the assigned course outcomes. It is as if they wrote their own learning guides and followed them. With each student devising a personal plan, there can be as many different plans and approaches in a classroom as there are students. Different students may study the process of erosion, for example, by reading about it, developing mathematical models, studying erosion in the field, conducting a computer search, consulting experts, or creating erosion models and reporting on their observations. This diversity requires two major course developments: the teacher must introduce a wide range of ways to learn and must organize an array of learning options for putting those ways to work. One way of introducing self-planning is to create several stations in the classroom, with each table offering alternative resources for dealing with one of the course outcomes. Students choose a table and then, from the resources and suggestions offered, design their own learning plans.

With program options in place, the teacher turns to developing a program to teach students how to find their strengths, plan their own learning activities, arrange their own resources, and launch their own initiatives. As student learning plans open up, they often include more concrete experiences as well as investigations, and both often lead to students' completing productive activities—a combination of experience, study, and action that we will call learning episodes. In this approach, the class becomes more like a workplace. Students work and interact with each other, while the teacher acts as enterprise supervisor. The teacher develops a planning format, introduces a procedure for negotiating action plans, and forges an agreement on criteria for success. The course may conclude with individual masterworks—in-depth studies leading to action and results—by each student in any field of choice.

Self-Directed Learning

In SDL, students choose their own outcomes; they decide what they will learn and how they will learn it. They design their own studies and activities and write up proposals that may be contracts with teachers and others about what they will achieve, the timetable they will follow, and the level of excellence they will seek. The teacher creates a framework for decisions, a support system to guide student progress, and a procedure to follow.

The framework for a course may be simply topics or themes, such as earth science, biology, chemistry, physics, and electronics or nonfiction, fiction, drama, poetry, and writing. If a whole school is involved, a broader infrastructure may include a pattern of individual challenges that students set for themselves in such areas as academic concentration, logical inquiry, practical applications, careers, adventure, service, or creativity. These may take students a year or more to achieve and may be required for graduation. The action plan or contract, timetables, and a working journal guide the student and assist the teacher in monitoring each student's work in progress.

Students need support, feedback, and help to be successful in SDL as in the rest of life. This is provided by the student's small peer support group, the larger teacher-led advisory group, conferences with the teacher, and possibly mentors at home and in the field. Learning options are often expanded to use such out-of-school resources as libraries, colleges, museums, apprenticeship sites, wilderness areas, and trips near and far. In SDL, motivation becomes critical: the student must find promising core interests and pursue them enthusiastically for their intrinsic values and their promise for the future.

The student plays a major role in assessment, negotiating standards, demonstrating achievement, and validating fieldwork. Teachers teach skills and processes, organize resources and contacts, and negotiate plans and guide student progress. Students may be charged with the full responsibility for planning, executing, and documenting their graduation studies in personal transcripts that go forward as their high school qualification. Anticipation of the real-life challenge of the graduation years is high motivation for students in the earlier grades.

How to Use the Stages

These four stages can be used in a number of different ways—for example,

- The teacher may use the stages as a menu for selecting strategies to introduce into the classroom.

- The teacher can select one stage to develop and pursue.

- The teacher or a group of teachers can use the stages as steps for systematically moving their students and themselves to SDL.

- The teacher may build a course by combining selected stages in SDL.

- A school may decide to use one stage as the major theme for each of the high school grades, ending with a challenge graduation year.

After deciding how they will pursue SDL, teachers move to the next step and develop the coursework. The curriculum required has three major themes: the learning activities students will undertake, the skills and processes involved, and the personal qualities that students must develop to meet their new responsibilities.

Linking the Stages to Grade Levels

Each of the four stages is a step further away from the TDL classroom. Each places a new demand on the student and the teacher. Each also opens up a new dimension of learning and a new level of responsibility.

When selecting the stage of SDL they will adopt, teachers should consider their students' state of readiness for SDL (see Resource B). They should consider also the freedom and the responsibility the program involves and the initiative and the determination it requires. Younger students may need a more gradual approach to SDL than do juniors and seniors, who are usually ready for the responsibility. For this reason, teachers in grades 8, 9, and 10 may find it more appropriate to begin with one or all of the first three stages, and teachers in grades 11 and 12 may find it more appropriate to move beyond the first stage , perhaps with an emphasis on graduation passages, which are challenges that students pursue in depth for up to a year or more. The intent is to move students to the greatest challenge in their lives and the most significant: a challenge that they set for themselves and that changes their lives.

The course can also be adapted by students themselves in seeking challenges that designate a level of difficulty that they can handle and in a style that suits them. All students are familiar with the lesson assignment–study–test–grade approach, and some are addicted to it, especially those who are successful at it. Still others will be so dependent or so afraid of independence that they cannot or dare not take any initiative. These are definitely impediments to SDL. They are also symptoms of an urgent need for it.

Students can learn to be self-directed at any age. Their capacity for self-direction varies greatly depending on their experience with it and their attitude toward it. Therefore, be prepared to take students into SDL gradually, teaching them the skills they need and first motivating them to learn under their own direction and then teaching them to motivate themselves. The bridging course discussed in the next section outlines a gradual approach. Be ready to provide diverse degrees of guidance. Be infinitely patient, and show unqualified respect. Your students will be struggling with the demons that keep them from taking responsibility for their learning, their lives, and themselves.

Different grades present different problems for adapting SDL. The differences arise primarily from the increased complexity in course content and the skills involved. Students in SDL can manage this increased complexity by first fulfilling assigned outcomes and then pursuing their own. A school can, however, accommodate the demands for new learning by both teachers and students by making each level of SDL a theme of one grade—for example,

Grade 8: Introduction to SDL Activities

Grade 9: Thinking Independently

Grade 10: Self-Managed Learning

Grade 11: Self-Planned Learning

Grade 12: Self-Directed Learning

Students of SDL may do a completely self-directed year, negotiating contracts for all of their activities without any reference to the required curriculum. (This is seldom possible in a public school.) Coursework, however, can usually be reduced to its essentials—some combination of English, math, science, and history or geography. Outcomes also vary. As SDL students develop more skills, outcomes can become more general to allow more latitude for choices. The outcome "To understand character development in Charlotte Bronte's *Pride and Prejudice*" can become "To understand character development in the novel" or "To study the novel" or simply "Literature." The most common form of SDL in schools is the completion of assigned topics and a series of challenges or passages designed to meet some additional requirements in such areas as creativity, adventure, academic concentration, research, career, personal development, service, or logical inquiry. The emphasis in these passages is "Challenge to the limit of my ability."

SDL can be taught to anyone at any age in any circumstances and in many different ways. Teachers can select ideas to integrate with their TDL work. They can choose one stage as their approach or use the stages to introduce SDL in their courses or as a graduated sequence from grade to grade. SDL can be offered as a course in which students pursue expertise in a field of personal interest so that they learn everything about something as well as something about everything. Teachers can agree to include certain aspects of SDL at each grade level. Imagine that all of grade 12 were self-directed and teachers in the other grades reorganized to prepare students for it!

Designating Course Outcomes

A course is usually defined by a curriculum guide, textbooks, and required tests. The learning to be covered in the course is often stated in a list of goals and objectives for the teacher to cover. What we need in order to lay the groundwork for SDL is a list of the things that students have to know or accomplish in order to complete the course. We can refer to these generically as *outcomes*. Detaching the course from the teacher's control and making it available as outcomes that students can pursue independently is the first step in developing an SDL course. With all of the outcomes listed, the teacher can then glean, combine, and add items to make the strongest list of fifteen to twenty-five outcomes possible. Since many of the outcomes derived from curricular materials will focus on content coverage, it is important for the teacher to translate the outcomes into formats that invite a variety of approaches. For example, a curricular goal such as "The student will read *To Kill a Mockingbird* and study the development of character in Scout" can be made more open as "Character in the contemporary American novel." This statement lacks several of the qualities we usually associate with well-stated goals and objectives, but it serves the purposes of SDL by enabling students to set their own goals—to choose the novel to read, the character to study, and the approach to studying it. As teachers create their course units around a few outcomes, they can also make sure that each group invites a variety of approaches. Here are a few of the many ways to express outcomes:

Knowledge: Content That Students Must Master

"Be able to explain the forces that led to the decline of the Roman Empire"

"Will understand tectonic plate theory"

"Will know the symbols in the Periodic Table"

Skills: Subject-Specific Performance Abilities That Students Must Acquire

"Can assess the authenticity of sources of information"

"Will be able to write a coherent paragraph"

"Will be able to solve first-degree, single-variable equations"

Tasks: Activities That Students Must Undertake

"Will construct a map showing the major voyages of discovery during the fifteenth and sixteenth centuries"

"Will provide a service for someone in need without expectation of reward"

"Will construct three machines with increasing degrees of mechanical advantage"

Experiences: Events That Students Must Observe or Participate In

"Will attend a live performance of a play by Shakespeare"

"Will shadow a worker in a field of interest"

"Will climb and rappel down a cliff face under expert supervision"

Competencies: Demonstrated Ability to Do Something or Get Something Done

"Will be able to conduct a scientific investigation to answer a question"

"Will be able to pursue and secure work systematically (inquiry, application, interview)"

"Will be able to converse socially in Spanish"

SDL Skills and Processes: Abilities Students Develop in Order to Perform SDL Tasks Well

"Students will be able to set appropriate goals for themselves"

"Will be able to conduct an investigation and find a defensible conclusion"

"Will find a personal passion and pursue it to a high level of skill"

Challenges or Passages: Major Achievements in Which Students Motivate Themselves to Achieve Their Best Possible Performance in Different Fields

"To identify an issue of concern [political, social, environmental, or legal, for example], take an informed position, and pursue it in an appropriate way"

"To choose a mode of creative expression and produce a product or products of quality"

"To conduct a personal, physical, or spiritual adventure"

When teachers state outcomes that they feel must be covered to complete a course, they tend to be specific, stating the objectives, the materials to be used, and the test of achievement. When teachers are teaching students to be self-directed, the outcomes are usually more general, so that each student can develop an individual approach to achieving them. As a result, the outcomes for course coverage tend to specify knowledge, skills, and tasks, while the outcomes for self-directed activities tend to outline the kinds of experiences, competencies, and challenges that students are required to undertake (see Exhibit 3.1).

A statement of specific outcomes derived from the course curriculum guide or textbook may read like this for a unit on geological land forms:

EXHIBIT 3.1

Course Outcomes

Course Coverage (Specific Description)	Self-Directed Learning (General Description)
• Knowledge	• Experiences
• Skills	• Competencies
• Tasks	• Challenges

By the end of this unit, the student will be able to ...

1. Describe the major landforms.
2. Explain the processes by which landforms are created.
3. Outline the history of tectonic plate movement.
4. Explain the dynamics of earthquakes, volcanic eruptions, and erosion.

The teacher then has the choice of specifying what the student will do to achieve each of these or to leave the approach to the student or to groups of students. The more experienced the students are in SDL, the more general the outcomes can be, providing as much opportunity and responsibility as possible for students to set their own specific goals and develop their own plans.

The most primitive approach to specifying the activities as part of the outcome is to divide the textbook and questions into units that students complete one at a time, then take the test, and move on to the next unit. The intent with SDL is to move as far beyond that approach as possible. One way is to ensure that different kinds of outcomes are included in the course: knowledge, skills, tasks, experiences, competencies, and challenges. Here are some examples showing how that can be done for a unit on genetics in middle school science:

Middle School Science Unit (Genetics)
- Knowledge: The student will understand the genetic code and its relationship to the assembly of different proteins.
- Skills: The student will be able to apply the principles of inheritance to basic Mendelian genetics.
- Tasks: The student will create a chart or other visual that shows the cause of different types of mutations.
- Experiences: The student will see and make comprehensive notes on *The Geometry of Life,* a video on the study of identical twins.
- Competencies: The student will be able to conduct a simple genetic experiment using fruit flies.

- Challenge: The student will select an issue in genetics—such as cloning or stem cell research—take an informed position, explain it scientifically, and then take action.

If these outcomes covered all that the science teacher wished to accomplish in the genetics section of the course, he or she could use them in many different ways. They could be turned into questions for the class to answer: "How are characteristics conveyed from one generation of plants to another?" Each outcome could be the topic of a learning package that outlined the work required to achieve the expected level of understanding. Students could develop their own learning plans for each outcome, or they could be permitted to develop their own study goals in the area of genetics, science, or logical inquiry. For a class skilled and experienced in SDL, the unit could simply be, "The student will demonstrate a working knowledge of genetics." Their success in developing personal goals and plans will still depend on a great deal of assistance, guidance, instruction, and support from their class, but the responsibility for learning will be theirs.

Notice that all of the outcomes for a unit or course can be turned into any one of the kinds of outcomes, producing a list that is all content, all skills, all tasks, all experiences, all competencies, or all challenges. Notice also that students can develop their own outcomes in all or any of these forms.

Sue Baker, a math teacher at Chemainus High School in Chemainus, British Columbia, suggests the following outcomes for a unit on measurement for students of tenth-grade math:

Tenth-Grade Math Unit (Measurement)
- Students will understand formulas for the surface area and volume of geometric figures, including cones, spheres, and cylinders.
- Students will determine the relationships among linear scale factors, the surface areas, and the volumes of similar figures and objects.
- Students will prepare a comprehensive formula summary sheet for reference.
- Students will use formulas to determine the surface area and volume of geometric figures, including cones, spheres, and cylinders.
- Students will be able to apply scale factors to a real-life application of their choice.

Rod MacVicar and Ruth Foster of Centennial School in Coquitlam, British Columbia, suggest these outcomes for a senior unit on water chemistry:

Twelfth-Grade Science Unit (Chemistry)

- Learn to conduct water chemistry tests (tests for such elements as oxygen, phosphorus, nitrogen, and potassium and tests for turbidity, pH, and coliform count).
- Select a creek, and conduct a complete array of tests on its water chemistry.
- From the data gathered, create a chemical profile of the creek, compare your profile to data archived by previous students, and draw conclusions about the environmental status of the creek.
- Study the web of interconnections among the water quality and the biology of the stream and its environs, including human activity.
- Environmental stewardship: Decide what action is required to increase the quality of the creek's water chemistry, and then pursue it.

Once the outcomes are stated comprehensively and in manageable numbers, the teacher can develop them in many different ways, giving students more and more responsibility for achieving them in groups and on their own.

Developing Self-Managed Course Units

In self-managed learning, students usually learn from packaged or computerized units, which they can complete at their own pace. Packages may be as simple as a list of textbook readings and exercises. They can also include a rich array of media experiences; electronic, community, and other resources; and such instructional options as conferences, seminars, and workshops to meet the needs of individual students.

As a course unfolds and students become skilled, the packages can offer them learning choices and opportunities to develop their own course guides and projects. The student works through the text, completes the related activities, and self-administers a test at the end of each unit or package. In this way, all students can proceed at a speed appropriate to their ability; they learn to manage their own study behavior, and the process frees the teacher to help those who need it, when they need it.

A package can be for a single outcome or a whole course. It contains all that a student needs to complete the activities listed in it. For an outcome in mathematics, for example, the package might include a videotaped explanation and examples, problems, equipment, and manipulables. A learning guide is included in the package and provides outcomes, activities, assessment procedure, and references. It is the centerpiece of the array of resources that it refers to: books, videos, CDs, lab equipment, charts, tests, seminars, and sites available in the classroom, school, or community.

An example of an SML will illuminate the features of well-developed packages and self-managed programs. Thomas Haney High School in Maple Ridge, British Columbia, enrolls a thousand students from grades 8 through 12. All students are in individualized programs, which they pursue by completing learning guides or packages for each subject at their own pace. Each morning, they file their learning plans for the day and then follow them, drawing on a variety of resources offered by the school: private and group study areas, labs, course lessons, seminars, and individual consultation with teachers. Students have many forms of support as they work. One teacher made a video at his dining room table using an overhead camera to shoot him working out an example of every mathematical operation covered in his packaged course. Students borrow it or make their own copies. Other teachers offer workshops to help students who are struggling and teach them in conventional ways until they are ready to work on their own again.

Teachers (every teacher is an adviser with an advisory group) consult with students as they set goals and monitor their progress in achieving them. As advocates of the students' pursuits, advisers negotiate with subject-area teachers and communicate with parents. Subject-area teachers prepare the learning guides that students work through, provide presentations and seminars, and are available for individual consultation. Noncertified instructional assistants are available for individual assistance in each subject-area resource center.

The structure of a packaged course also enables teachers and students to introduce alternatives to the work assigned in learning guides. The faculty decided to standardize each course at twenty learning guides. Students can apply to use their own approaches to achieving course outcomes. They are invited to design projects to replace one, or as many as nine, of the guides (a suggested standard is five hours of work per guide on the average, or forty-five hours of work for a 9LG project—one equivalent to work on nine learning guides). Physics and math teachers at Thomas Haney invite students to undertake projects individually or in groups. Here are some examples of projects offered by Steve Grant, Dave McIntosh, and Jeff Radom, who teach grades 9 to 12 in the Sciences Department:

- Projectile launcher: Build a device that will launch an object a specific distance or height.

- Rocket construction: Build a rocket to lift off from the earth's surface and climb as high as possible without using explosives of any kind.

- Fluid dynamics: Demonstrate how the laws of motion in physics apply to the dynamic environment surrounding a river or other body of water.

Students are also encouraged to negotiate credit toward two or more courses for extensive work on any learning guide. A student making a case for conserving a wilderness environment, for example, may study the area, review its history, and make a case for conserving it. She may then apply for credits in science, social studies, and English. A program in which students work independently at their own rates is also more open to field trips by individuals, groups, or classes. A cross-curricular grade 8 team at Thomas Haney is offering an integrated math, social studies, English, and science program, making use of a nearby park and river basin.

Thomas Haney is a member of the Canadian Coalition of Self-Directed Learning centered at Bishop Carroll High School in Calgary, Alberta. Bishop Carroll participated in the Model Schools Project (MSP) and is the only Canadian member of the Coalition of Essential Schools. The MSP is based on the Trump Plan, a program proposed by J. Lloyd Trump (1977) to combine options for learning with guidance on choosing among them well. The plan's five key features are the teacher adviser role, independent study, individualized scheduling, continuous progress, and differentiated staffing. The packages at Thomas Haney take many different forms. Exhibit 3.2 is an example of one approach.

From this learning guide, we can see both what teachers must do to prepare their courses and what students must learn to do in order to fulfill their responsibilities successfully. The SML teacher decides on the outcomes, the activities, and the means of assessment, while the student must develop the skills of self-management to undertake and successfully complete the activities assigned.

EXHIBIT 3.2

Eleventh-Grade Earth Sciences Learning Guide (Earth's Structure and Tectonics)

ROCKS AND MINERALS

Introduction

The study of earth materials—rocks and minerals—introduces you to the physical components of our planet and their importance as resources for society.

Learning Guide Outcomes

On completion of this Learning Guide, you will be able to:

1. Differentiate between rocks and minerals.
2. Use physical and chemical properties to identify and classify selected rocks and minerals.

EXHIBIT 3.2 (continued)

3. Describe the formation of igneous, sedimentary, and metamorphic rocks, and relate them to the rock cycle.

4. Classify rocks as igneous, sedimentary, and metamorphic using texture and composition.

5. Describe the relationship between crystal size and cooling rate in igneous rocks.

6. Classify igneous rocks as volcanic (extrusive) or plutonic (intrusive) on the basis of texture.

7. Recognize ways in which the study of rocks relates to local geology and industries.

8. Correlate rock units from one area to another.

Evaluation

1. Activity 2: Mineral Identification Lab

2. Activity 3: Practical Test

Resources

1. Text: *Earth Science,* Chapter 4

2. Video: *Minerals—Building Blocks of the Earth* or suitable substitute from the kiosk

3. Geology Mineral Project, pp. L2–L6

4. Mineral lab kit

Learning Activities

Activity 1   Rock or Mineral?   1 hour

- Review the information in your text Heath *Earth Science,* pp. 29–41.
- Give complete answers in your notebook to Topic Questions 8–12 on p. 37 and question 15, p. 41.
- View the video *Minerals—Building Blocks of the Earth,* which may be obtained from the Humanities kiosk. Write a summary of the main points made in the video.

Activity 2   Mineral Identification Lab   2 hours

- Carefully read the information in your text Heath *Earth Science,* Chapter 4: "How to Know the Minerals," pp. 47–57.
- Note: READ ALL THE INFORMATION BELOW AND IN THE LISTED EXERCISE BEFORE YOU BEGIN!
- From the Earth Science 11 files, obtain a copy of the Geology Mineral Project: Student Exercise package, pp. L2–L6. Your task is to construct a chart similar to that shown in your text on p. 59 but which contains each of the categories listed on p. L2 of your exercise package.
- A set of 20 minerals will be available to you from the science resource center. You will be responsible for identifying the physical properties of these minerals. Do not break or cleave any of these minerals.
- Complete each of the tests as described in the Student Exercise package and complete your chart. Work must be neat and complete.

Activity 3   Practical Mineral Identification Test   15 minutes

- Make an appointment with your instructor to set up a mineral identification test. You will be shown a number of samples and within a limited time period be able to identify them.

Bring your completed activities with you to the seminar for this guide.

Source: *Developed by earth sciences teachers George McRae and Jeff Radom of Thomas Haney High School. Reprinted with the permission of Thomas Haney High School, Maple Ridge, British Columbia, Canada.*

Student-Planned Coursework and Projects

Students are often assigned projects that they design and undertake independently or in teams. At Island Pacific School on Bowen Island in British Columbia, for example, students graduating from grade 9 conduct a masterwork in a field of their own choice. A masterwork is a major undertaking, such as a study of local history, an investigation into environmental pollution, or an exhibition of metal sculpture. At graduation, students present their results and describe their learning experience to an audience of peers, teachers, parents, and other members of the community. To complete such projects, students need to learn the skills required for goal setting, project design, and often self-assessment. In other classes in other schools, the student-designed project is often the final activity in an otherwise teacher-directed course and is an application of course concepts and practices.

Cathy Lee Hwa, an English teacher, creates frameworks for individual studies or projects. She chooses such topics for her units as change, natural learning, character, and the hero's journey. She frames out the issues and relates them to literature and other art forms. She brings in books, videos, and works of art to illustrate her points and open up possibilities. The possibilities are recorded on a web that becomes a menu for student choices later. In her change unit, for example, she introduces technological change with snippets from a video on the Wright brothers' struggle to achieve powered flight in 1903, then a segment from the movie *The Right Stuff* based on the Tom Wolfe book, and finally a sequence from *Close Encounters of the Third Kind* so that the past, present, and future implications of technological change will be discussed. In a similar way, she introduces other changes in technology, discovery, individual rights, and knowledge about ourselves and the world.

To equip students for assignments such as this one, Hwa teaches them three skills: goal setting, planning, and assessment. Goal setting involves selecting a theme of interest, exploring the possibilities offered by that theme, and then choosing the best possibility, that is, the one most desirable from the students' point of view. Next, she teaches students how to state their choices as goals that will act as clear guides to what they intend to do. For example, some students who pursue the theme of change choose topics that she has already introduced, like flight and women's rights. Others discover their own topics, such as genetics, political freedom, or warfare. Still others choose changes in and through music, literature, or art. When students present their descriptions of change and the impact changes have on society, each of them fleshes out the main theme. Many questions are answered in this way, but many more are raised, which is just the way Hwa planned it. The skills she taught are fleshed out in Exhibit 3.3.

EXHIBIT 3.3

Teaching Students to Design Their Own Learning

Goal Setting

- Identify a topic, theme, or field.
- Generate aspects of the topic to study.
- Select an aspect, and express it as a goal.

Planning

- List the resources on hand or accessible.
- Generate a list or web of activities for reaching your goal.
- Organize these activities into a coherent procedure, story, or pathway.
- Use reverse or straight-ahead planning.

Assessment

- Arrange for regular feedback on your progress.
- Decide how you will prove your learning success and demonstrate your achievement.
- State the criteria by which your work will be judged.

Students receive the sheet or booklet with the outcome and a list of options for achieving it. Each student designs a personal approach, writes up a plan, submits it for approval, negotiates an acceptable final form, and then completes the work and demonstrates completion in the agreed-on way. Students may conduct one outcome, one unit, or a whole course in this manner. Completing two or three as a class and then two or three more in small groups helps students to develop the skills and a pattern for success.

Focusing on Competencies and Challenges

A curriculum can be defined in a list of the competencies students are expected to develop. A competency is the ability to perform well in a specified field of activity. For example, students may be expected to develop a competency in solving quadratic equations, leading small groups, or performing before an audience. Competencies often include skill, attitude, and know-how. A competency in leading small groups, for example, involves group skill, but also relationships with group members, the ability to solve problems, and the capacity to get the group task done. Competencies are revealed in performance and assessed by demonstration. Expressing a curriculum in competencies offers a flexible approach for both teachers and students. Teachers can express as competencies both their course outcomes and outcomes designed to offer students a wider range of choice. An English teacher may list such required outcomes as, "The student can express an opinion about a work of literature and support it with convincing evidence," and then add such open competencies for students as, "The student can write creatively in a literary form to an acceptable level of quality." Students can attain the competencies by taking classes, following learning guides, or writing proposals for activities they design themselves.

One framework for the student pursuit of excellence is a series of challenges that students set for themselves as part of their graduation passage. A demanding competency is a challenge; a personally transforming challenge is a passage. Passages can be assigned as early as the beginning of grade 11 and can be introduced with a range of prechallenge activities—briefer, less demanding events that allow students to practice for the demanding work ahead. If "Adventure" is one of the challenge areas, for example, students may be introduced to a range of adventure activities: rock climbing, river rafting, or long-distance running, for example. The inner adventure, or exploration of one's self, that matches the outer adventure will be explored. Personal adventures will become a topic of discussion in advisory and support groups. Students will plan prechallenge adventures, and as their own challenge adventures take shape, they will begin to prepare their proposals for presentation to a special meeting of their advisory group. The students are building the most valuable and most impressive transcripts—dossiers of their activities and achievements—they can create for presentation at graduation and later to prospective employers. The SDL framework is designed to enable every student to excel. Resource C shows students how to handle the passage process.

Students of Jefferson County Open address several levels of challenge. First, they are challenged to achieve twenty-seven competencies, referred to as "expectations." This list includes competence in basic subject areas, but goes further into personal, social, survival, and career skills: "the ability to engage in honest self-evaluation," "a willingness to take appropriate risks," "the ability to define values and make moral decisions," and "the ability to think clearly and solve problems effectively." Students can propose any promising approach to achieving these competencies and meeting these expectations. Courses are offered to help students complete the basics, and once students declare class involvement, they are required to attend that class. Many other approaches are possible, such as the ones chosen for completing the math competency over the years, which include taking an on-site, Internet, or college math course; conducting practical math work; or mounting a project involving math. Another approach for students is to propose teaching a course of their own in the subject. Jason, for example, taught a course on dinosaurs and the Jurassic Period to several other eighth-grade students and received favorable reviews.

Second, they are challenged to challenge themselves to major achievements in six areas: logical inquiry, practical applications, creativity, service, career explorations, and adventure. These are major activities: students write proposals and present them to their support groups and their advisory groups. Once their proposals are approved, they undertake them. Once the proposals are completed, they present their achievements to an audience of peers, teachers, parents, other adult contacts, and members of the community. These presentations are their final graduation requirement. The completion of their basic competencies and their six challenges is listed in the transcript compiled by the student, along with proof that each has been completed and the student's testimony about the significance and accomplishment involved in them.

Teachers provide a number of activities designed to assist students in completing their competencies and challenges. The most celebrated among students are trips and apprenticeships. Every student is involved in planning, funding, and organizing at least one trip to an important site that can become the focus for various challenges. It may include a service trip to help farmers in a distant state to dig out from under a recent flood, or a trip to an archaeological site in Mexico or to literary sites in England. Apprenticeships are career related and cover all fields from theater to architecture. Here are some examples of challenges that students have undertaken:

Logical Inquiry

- After the events of September 11, 2001, Ramzi began an inquiry into the nature of terrorism and its relationship to the Islamic religion.

- Carla did service work at an earthquake site and decided to find out what caused the earthquake and how others can be predicted.

- Chad became interested in chaos theory and began an investigation into its nature and application.

Practical Application

- Stan began recording a rock group's music and decided to study recording and to build a recording studio at home from used equipment.

- Karen wanted to row competitively and studied how to achieve maximum health, strength, and performance.

- Balbir studied how to start a small business, traced three from their start through difficulties to success, and designed his own business plan.

Creative Expression

- Eleanor and four other girls with dancing backgrounds created a troupe, choreographed a modern dance, and presented it at school and in several other venues.

- Maxine became interested in the plight of children working in factories, and developed a presentation on what her life would be like under the conditions those children experienced. She presented it to service groups to raise money for relief.

- Aki learned pottery from a relative and presented a display of his work.

Service

- Meli looked after her dying grandmother for three months.

- Damon worked in a soup kitchen every week.

- Phyllis, with the help of two friends, started a recycling service in her neighborhood.

Career Explorations

- Geraldine shadowed an architect and arranged an apprenticeship in the office.

- Brooke worked as an assistant to the cooks in the school cafeteria.

- Drew taught English to a small group of children of recent immigrants.

Adventure

- Several students cited a school rafting trip as their adventure.

- Morgan, along with two friends, studied the explorations of Lewis and Clark and followed a section of their travels to the Pacific.

- Adele studied Buddhism and entered a nearby monastery for several study sessions and retreats.

Students are assisted in their decisions about their proposals and in planning for them by their peer support groups and then by a teacher-led advisory group. Parents are often included in negotiations, and their approval is required for any out-of-school activities. Students demonstrate their achievements to peers and others, and their achievements are celebrated.

• • •

Courses are the frameworks for lessons. How do teachers plan lessons for SDL? We turn to that question next.

Chapter 4

Planning Lessons and Projects

TEACHING SDL means dramatic changes in the way teachers teach and the way students learn. While there is some truth in the worn adage that the teacher shifts from being "the sage on the stage" to becoming "the guide on the side," successful SDL teaching is not just differentiated. It requires a full spectrum of approaches, ranging from instruction to counseling.

Principles for Planning Lessons

- *Teach students the skills they need to take control over their learning activities.* The basic guideline in teaching for SDL is the transfer of control from the teacher to the student. The major transfer is control over the learning process: over how to learn, when to learn, the pace of learning, where the learning takes place, and what is learned and why. This shift in the locus of control also involves developing students' awareness of becoming inner directed. This practice depends on reflective thinking—the students' ability to think about who they are and their abilities, interests, and goals. Shifting control to students involves giving them new freedoms and responsibilities, both of which can be difficult and intimidating. The teacher not only transfers control but also helps students recognize, accept, and manage these new circumstances.

- *Shift the emphasis of the program from content to productivity.* One major switch in the move from TDL to SDL is from an emphasis on recall to an emphasis on productivity. In the teacher-directed classroom, the content is presented by the teacher, students are assigned study or practice work, and then they take a test on the material they studied and practiced. In SDL, the shift is away from this directive approach to one in which students discover their own purposes, set their own learning goals, and then develop plans for reaching them successfully. In the TDL class, the teacher presents a lesson on astronomy focused on the solar system. Then students typically read a chapter from the textbook and do assigned questions in preparation for the weekly test. In SDL, in contrast, one student may decide to make a telescope so that he can examine the planets and the stars. He would plan a step-by-step process for making the telescope and then put it into action. The switch is from lesson–study–test to goal–plan–outcome.

• *Introduce new practices in gradual gradients of complexity.* It is important to phase in new practices gradually. One way to do that is to increase the gradient of intensity slowly. The rule of gradients says that students do better at mastering new skills, new responsibilities, and new levels of performance in SDL when they are introduced to them gradually. Increased intensity means increased complexity, difficulty, risk, involvement, and responsibility. Each gradient of intensity in SDL requires new levels of understanding, skill, feeling, performance, and commitment. Begin with the simple, easy, and safe; progress systematically to the complex, difficult, and risky. Practice as a class, then in groups, and finally as individuals. Be sure that students are introduced to new tasks at steadily increasing gradients of intensity.

• *Make new ideas familiar by connecting them to students' lives.* Students understand new ideas best when they are connected to their own experiences. For that reason, teachers increase their effectiveness when they connect unfamiliar ideas they are presenting with familiar touchstones in the students' own lives. SDL is ideally suited to this principle because the projects students develop for themselves grow naturally from their own experience. Such touchstones of familiarity can be of three kinds: remembered past experiences, ongoing current activities, or possible experiences in the future.

These touchstones of familiarity play an important role in SDL. The past is a treasure chest of lessons about what works and what does not. The students' current reality tells them what they need and offers them a feast of opportunities to learn. The future is an array of possibilities, and the vision of the future they desire is a beacon to guide them. Connections with the past, present, and future make learning perennial and powerful.

• *Develop in students the attitudes necessary for success.* Students require a spectrum of positive attitudes to be successful in SDL: interest, confidence, determination, courage, and especially self-efficacy. Efficacy, according to Albert Bandura (1977, p. 79), "is the conviction that one can successfully execute the behavior required to produce the outcomes" desired. How important is it to develop a sense of personal effectiveness? Bandura expresses the answer clearly: "The strength of people's convictions in their own effectiveness determines whether they will even try to cope with difficult situations," and the best way to develop this powerful conviction is through "experiences of mastery arising from successful performance" (p. 79). That performance is achieved best through guided practice. Such attitudes can also be nurtured, according to Martin Seligman (1990), when people learn to be optimistic. They can do that by learning to intervene when their inner dialogues become negative and make them more positive by changing the inner message from "I can't do this" to "I can nail this challenge." Success in SDL operates on these attitudes of self-efficacy. From the beginning, every aspect of the program should contribute to its cultivation.

• *Change from telling to asking, from lecturing to interaction.* Teachers are used to telling. They are captains, and students the crew; order, direction, and obedience are essential for the success of the mission—great for marching students through their TDL paces, but not so good for cultivating self-direction. Teachers are most helpful when they help students to decide for themselves rather than decide for them. Helping students to help themselves is best accomplished in a productive conversation that moves constructively toward the clarification of an idea, the solution to a problem, or the acceptance of a proposal. "This is the answer, and this is how you get it," the telling teacher says. "What is your question, and how do you think you could go about figuring out the answer?" asks the asking teacher, beginning a productive conversation.

• *Launch the student on a hero's journey of discovery.* In SDL, we launch our students on the hero's journey, which is both inward and outward. Students leave the easy and familiar to face the challenging and unknown. In their adventure, they face not only the risky struggle to be successful but also the struggle to overcome fear, doubt, and the chaos within. Like Theseus entering the labyrinth to face the Minotaur, they begin their challenges—perhaps the construction of a robot, an apprenticeship in an architect's office, or running a boil of river rapids—to accomplish the tasks they have set and to deal with the feelings involved when they confront themselves in demanding situations. We urge them to go out far and in deep, and when they do, the prize is twofold: accomplishment and insight about themselves. With both, the student is transformed.

The gap between TDL and SDL is a significant one. Bridging it requires a paradigm shift in perspective on learning and schooling by both teacher and student. For this reason, many teachers may prefer to make the switch gradually, over the duration of a particular course or over several forms of the course or program they are teaching. This process enables them to master the appropriate approaches systematically and to develop a preferred way to introduce students to the SDL process.

Designing Learning Episodes

Learning episodes are a coherent series of activities related to an organizing idea or intention that may occur anywhere. In SDL, they have three main elements: experience, study, and productive activity. It is easy to think of them in a sequence of inciting experience, leading to profound study, leading to inspired productivity, and certainly episodes may unfold in such a sequence, but they can occur in any order. All three dimensions can be compressed into a single event, or they can all focus on only one of the three elements. Here are a few examples of experience, study, and productive activity:

- Mark hears a poet read her poems, reads more of her work, and decides to write poetry.

- Allison reads *Galileo's Daughter* and becomes fascinated by the struggle between science and the church, evidence and revelation. She studies the period and makes a video of a conversation between Galileo and the pope.

- The teacher heats a little water in a gallon tin container until the steam in it swells its sides. Suddenly, he plunges the tin into a basin of ice and water. As the tin collapses and twists as if being wrung, it makes a scream like a cranked guitar amplifier. The class is stunned. The teacher asks, "What questions does this raise, and how can we answer them?" After the discussion, the students produce a chart they title "The Gas Laws."

- The landlord lives in the apartment next to the one where Marjory and her mother live. He had begun to let himself in to their apartment to demand more money and to threaten them with eviction if they did not pay. Marjorie goes to the library, studies the law, contacts Legal Aid, and then coaches her mother for a meeting with the landlord. Marjory has learned that the landlord could be arrested if he comes into the apartment uninvited again, that they could take liberties redecorating, and that they would be very difficult to evict. The landlord withdraws.

- Fred visits an archaeological dig on a school trip, studies local archaeology, and finds a place working on a nearby dig. Using the experience for his passage in logical inquiry, he shows a videotape and describes life in an ancient native village.

We turn now to examine each of the three components of the learning episode—experience, study, and productivity—which are summarized in Table 4.1. The activities involved in each cell of the integrated learning unit are set out in Resource D.

TABLE 4.1

The Integrated SDL Learning Unit

	Experience	Study	Productivity
Personal	Deepening awareness of oneself and one's personal view of the world	Learning about oneself, developing strengths, pursuing interests, clarifying values, cultivating characters	Developing oneself through challenging pursuit of personal goals
Social	Experience in social interaction with a diverse array of other people	Increasing knowledge about relationships, group interaction, and how to function socially	Creates skill in working with others in a variety of roles in different forms of activity
Technical	Expanding experience of the world in all of its forms	Increasing knowledge about the world, how it works, and how to function in it	Greater ability to function in the world: accumulating competence and achievements

In TDL the emphasis is usually on study activities in the technical domain, while in SDL the focus broadens. Study is grounded in experience, and both lead to productive action. Achievement in the technical domain is balanced with personal and social development. In SDL, all of these fields and domains are integrated into a single unit of study. Students learn about themselves, others, and the world through experience, studies, and productive activities. Another dynamic is also at work in each cell of Table 4.1: inflow and outflow. In each element of the unit, students are both receptive and generative, that is, they receive experience, studies of what is known, and assigned activities, but they also create experiences, conduct investigations, and initiate action. Learning episodes are one basic way to teach integrated learning units.

Creating Experiences

Experience is our most often used pathway to learning and plays many roles (see Figure 4.1). Watershed experiences are a continuing course of stimulation and often have a profound influence on our lives. Exciting experiences command our attention and provoke us with wonder and curiosity. Extensive and repeated experience can make us wise; if it is practice, it can make us competent. How much we learn from the experience depends on both the richness of it and our capacity to perceive it. Learning, writes

FIGURE 4.1

Dimensions of Experience

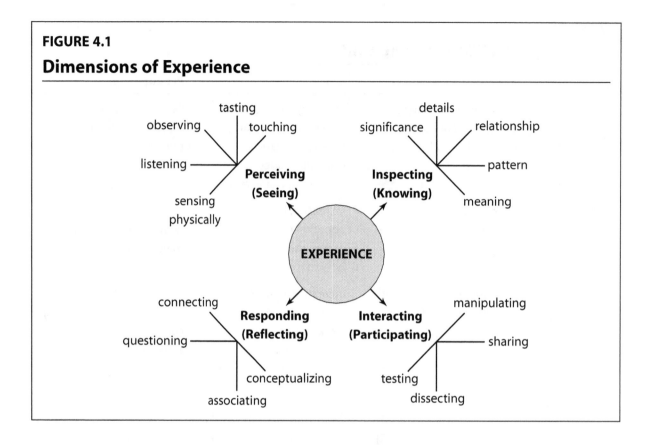

David Kolb (1984), "is the process whereby knowledge is created through the transformation of experience" (p. 38).

Some people pass through an art gallery and see nothing; others see the universe in a grain of sand. "What do you see?" asked the director of the laboratory, pointing to the fish that the young lab assistant had been studying for a week. When he finished his answer, the director shook his head and sent him back to work. He returned in three weeks and when he reported, the director said, "At last you are beginning to see." Learning to see is one part of learning to experience. Every degree of awareness we acquire opens another level of the world to us; first there is awareness, then understanding, then we are face to face with the unknown.

Experience both teaches and provokes. The task for the teacher is, first, to provide provocative experiences and to teach students to learn from them, and, second, to teach students to seek out and learn from experiences themselves. The key is connection with the phenomenon at hand, pausing to see and wonder. The student strips the bark from a stump and sees the citronella ants scurrying away and wonders, "Where are they going, and what will they do in those dark recesses of the wood?" Years later, that boy—Edward O. Wilson—became the world's leading authority on ants and the founder of sociobiology. He continues to ask those questions.

Not all experiences are watersheds of wonder, but experiences can and should have the potential to stimulate. Whenever possible, experiences should be direct, that is, they should place students in touch with the real thing. And when that is not possible, the experience should be made as direct as possible by bringing the experience into the classroom or representations of it through media or demonstrations. Active participation by students increases the connection. Direct provocation can also be created with simulated situations, problems, paradoxes, and questions. Drama intensifies. The teacher who reported experiencing the screeching, twisting metal container as a student recalled it forty-five years later. The central desired outcome from such events is wonder and questions that must be answered—for example,

- Mrs. Margolis took her class to the city art gallery and invited them to look through the gallery to find the one painting or sculpture that grabbed them more than any other. Then she said to go back to it and look it over closely until it became "a friend." Later, she invited volunteers to take the class to their piece and talk about it.

- When Amir saw a movie about the effect of pollution on people in a town near a factory, he began to worry about his own town and took his friends on a hike to look for signs of that possibility.

- Ms. Prevost posed this question to her class: "How can we communicate with others by saying what we do not mean?" After a discussion, she asked a pair of prepared students to model irony, sarcasm, and satire in brief dialogues, after which students wrote dramatic conversations using these expressions.

Promoting Study

Study is the organized pursuit of answers to questions that matter. It takes many forms, which are essentially ways to investigate. In teaching students the craft of study, it is important that they learn both the content under study and the enduring skills of pursuing it. The first step is to find essential questions. These often derive directly from the stimulating experience. Still, the question must be identified from many possibilities and then clarified to specify exactly what is being asked. Some students are naturally curious and excited about learning; others must learn to energize their questions with emotion by tapping into their interests, becoming curious, and visualizing the possibilities of the inquiry to follow.

The inquiry begins by gathering information from a number of different possible sources, including print, other media, the Internet, people, and direct investigative experiences. This information is then sorted and organized into categories for explanation and interpretation. Finally, a coherent answer to the question is prepared for a presentation both of the answer and why it is appropriate. The result we seek is understanding and contribution to our unfolding knowledge. Grant Wiggins and Jay McTeghe, in *Understanding by Design* (1998), describe many useful approaches to this stage in the process.

Investigation is only a stage in the learning episode. When Wilbur and Orville Wright took on the question, "How can we make a machine that will fly?" they began by studying everything they could find on flight and contacting authorities who could help them. Study was preliminary to conceptualization, experimentation, and, finally, productivity. Experimentation is modeled on the scientific method and is a way of testing emerging ideas or seeking out new information. Based on the results of experiences, inquiries, and experiments, students translate their searches into concepts that will become elements of their understanding and formulations of the world (see Figure 4.2).

All of these aspects of study require skills in research, analysis, and evaluation. As they are needed, these skills should be taught. During many uses, the skills will be practiced and perfected. Concepts developed in this manner will be remembered, and the skills developed will be tools for a life of learning. Here are a few examples of studies carried out by students:

FIGURE 4.2

Dimensions of Study

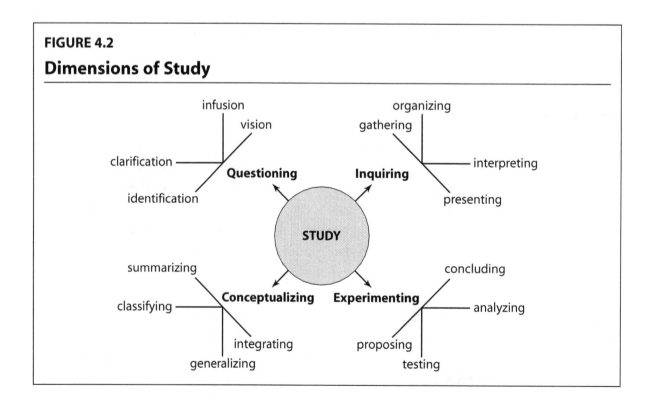

- Mr. Yee asked his students if the American revolutionaries who won freedom from British control shared any features with the recent revolutionaries who were in the streets protesting the meetings of world leaders in Seattle, Genoa, and Quebec. They conducted an investigation together.

- Jean decided to find out how wireless electronic instruments such as cell phones work.

- Vincent became interested in the application of statistics to the study of social problems and gathered data from students on bullying: how often it occurs, attitudes toward it, causes of it, and incidence of it among students of different ages. His report was used by the district authorities.

Encouraging Productivity

SDL moves regularly and steadily toward productivity with its own kind of knowledge, its own set of skills, and outcomes that demonstrate competence. Through productive activities, students learn to find and develop their own strengths and interests. From them, students develop the directions they wish to follow both within course boundaries and beyond them in pursuit of personal visions of excellence. They learn to plan, organize, and execute the practical skills required to make things happen. These skills are translatable to any course and any life activity that requires intentional action. They are the tools that anyone needs to direct their own lives and make their aspirations a reality. Here are a few examples of student productivity:

- Choy's English class published a magazine containing a poem, story, brief essay, or work of art by every student, with a foreword by the teacher. The students turned the class into an editorial room and produced the magazine using their computers and printer.

- Miguel built a model of a lever, and so did his friends Philippa and Carl. They suggested that the class build a physics display of examples of gears, pulleys, and levers to explain mechanical advantage. Someone suggested inviting another class in. Someone else suggested an exchange of explanatory displays about various aspects of physics with another class.

- Sandra became interested in design after attending a fashion show and began designing her own clothes. A part of her graduation performance was a show of her line modeled by classmates.

The emphasis in productive activity is on process, the sequence of steps—each one often requiring a new skill—that leads to a demonstrable outcome.

FIGURE 4.3

Aspects of Productivity

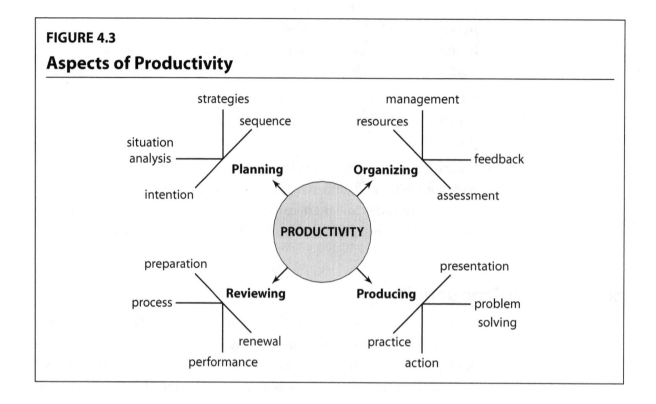

Figure 4.3 outlines the basic process. In the first stage, students search for a focus. In coursework, this means creating a chemistry in the mix of personal orientation—strengths, interests, and experience—and the demands of the program. The experiences and studies that have gone before often give students many opportunities to generate ideas for further pursuits. During prior stages, students, knowing that generative activity lies ahead, can be prompted to consider what questions they might try to answer and what initiatives they might undertake. Students can also benefit from learning to visualize, and by developing a vision of the future they desire, or more specifically, the best they can imagine creating. Sometimes, of course, the answer is more study. There is a central mental or emotional state implicit in each stage of productivity, too (see Resource E). In focusing, it is clarity, the student's need to cut through the chaos of adolescence and find the core of his own nature, concerns, and interests. The need for clarification is one reason that negotiation with students about their intentions is so important.

Involving Students in Project Planning

Once the focus is clear, students can set their goals and begin to consider how to reach them. Planning their approach is as challenging for students as planning courses and lessons is for the teacher, which is why the rule of functional equivalents is so important: every time you stop a form of teacher direction (such as goal setting or planning), teach students how to do it for themselves. They have to analyze the situation, that is, size up what is required, what is available, and whether it is accessible. How much preparation does ocean scuba diving require? Are the local waters suitable? Is training available? What is the cost? If the circumstances are navigable, then the student can proceed to generate ideas about how to get the job done, formulating strategies for action and placing them in a sequence to follow. Once a plan is completed, the next step is to organize the requirements for putting the plan into action: gathering the resources necessary, scheduling time, arranging for feedback about progress, and deciding how success will be determined. Finally, it is time to act. Practicing the skills required may be the main item. Action itself is complex and demanding. It requires initiative and determination, not to mention the exercise of skills in real situations with real consequences. Above all, students must become skilled problem solvers to overcome the inevitable glitches and obstacles so that they can achieve their goals.

This is the action process that is outlined in student contracts, their formal proposals for projects. In many cases, student plans will include experiences and studies they need in order to get their work done, that is, they may often plan a complete learning episode.

Experience, study, and productivity are the three major ways of learning and knowing. Experience, laden with sensory stimulation that has an inexhaustible potential for insight, offers the individual the opportunity to know by the personal perception of significance. We can nevertheless be in the presence of phenomena and experience little. The task of the teacher is to teach students to see, to connect and find meaning through reflection about what is perceived. The challenge is to move perception over time to greater range and depth. Experience not only yields greater awareness and explicit knowledge; it also feeds intuition.

Study is the pursuit of conceptual knowledge based on evidence and confirmed by proof. It is a rigorous process that involves focus on a question or issue, research into what is known, and experiment or investigation to test ideas or gather new evidence. The challenge for the teacher is to guide students through the evidence gathered and to help them construct concepts or examine and reconstruct worn-out ones. The intent is to develop in them an inquiring attitude of mind and to make them skilled in the process so that they can apply it on their own in their own quest for understanding and knowledge.

Productive activity involves the search for meaning through action. The student learns to focus effort, plan for a successful venture, and then enact it. In that process, there is much to learn as well as to achieve: every initiative is an experiment from which we can learn. Students learn the process involved in taking action systematically and learn from the action that they take. From the way they manage the process and the action itself, they learn a great deal about themselves and the realm in which they have worked. Often, we act and move on. The task of the teacher is to teach students to maintain an ongoing study of their activities and in the end to review what they learned from the process, about the field in which they worked, and about themselves as productive people. On the basis of their conclusions, they may also review where they are and where they want to go next. Reflection, conceptualization, and review are ways of seeking answers to the question "What did I learn here?" and in the shadow of that question, "What do I want to learn or do next?"

Teaching learning episodes is an excellent way to prepare students for other forms of SDL. Experiment, study, and especially action prepare students to conduct successful projects, challenges, and all other forms of SDL.

Note that in all three of these ways of learning, students are not learning just process and content. They are also learning about themselves in a kind of mega-metacognition. They are not just thinking and not just thinking about thinking (metacognition), but thinking about themselves as perceivers, thinkers, and performers (mega-metacognition). The questions—Who am I? How well am I doing? Where am I going? Who do I want to become? and What do I want to accomplish?—are always in the air. These three stages of an SDL learning episode offer many opportunities for teachers to help students to examine themselves as independent, self-directed people.

Here are examples of applying the episode format: one by a student and another by a teacher.

Teacher-Directed Episode Format

Outcome: The development of appreciation and critical sensibility in literature.

General comment: Mr. Roberts focuses his literature class on writing. The class is organized for different forms of publication. For fiction and nonfiction, they set up as the *Los Angeles Book Review*, patterned on the *New York Review of Books*. This episode focuses on poetry, including song lyrics.

Experience: Mr. Roberts brought into class as many books, CDs, videotapes, and audiotapes of poetry as he could gather. He invited students to add to the collection, including CDs of songs they considered to be interesting poetry. After an introduction to poetry, during which he presented two of his own selections, he assigned each student to read, listen to, and watch in search of the best poems they could find. This was the raw material for what would become their personal collections.

Study: Mr. Roberts introduced the question, "What distinguishes a good poem from an average one?" He combined what he called "jotting" with discussion. Students made brief notes on their answers illustrated from their personal selections and then discussed their responses as a class. In the summary, they identified two lists: one of the elements in good poetry and one of the criteria that distinguishes good poetry from bad. Students next chose two poems from their selections (or new ones that they wanted to include after the discussion) and wrote critical appreciations about them.

Productivity: Students produced both a personal collection and a class collection. Each student assembled the best poems from those he or she had gathered, wrote a critical introduction, and published them, often with illustrations. In small groups, students reviewed their collections and submitted selected poems to an editorial team for the class collection. One group decided to make a poem-video based on the approach used in music videos, and the other groups followed. A few students produced collections of poems they had written. Students exchanged collections, offered copies of their class collection for sale to others, and produced a noon-hour program of their poem videos.

Student-Directed Learning Episode

Ireni is a grade 9 student in a humanities class. This is one of her learning episodes.

Experience: Ireni searched for a question to jump-start her learning episode. One Sunday, she and her family visited her favorite aunt, Judith, who was dying from emphysema. Ireni was shocked to see her so ill and still smoking. When she asked her aunt why she hadn't stopped smoking, she could not make sense of Aunt Judith's answer: "The doctors don't know what they're talking about. I've been smoking all my life." The smoke and the coughing and the denial made a profound impression on Ireni. She had been tempted to smoke; many of her friends had already begun. Now, a number of questions formed in Ireni's mind: "What makes people smoke? Does smoking really cause diseases? If so, are there cures?" That wasn't a single question, but she discussed it in the advisory group and decided it was a suitable cluster to work with.

Study: Ireni laid out a plan to become informed and answer her questions. She decided to visit the cancer clinic, to go on-line, and to visit the library to gather the resources she needed. Her friend Tonya suggested calling her father, a doctor who "is death on smoking!" Ireni discovered peer pressure and advertising attract people to smoking, and nicotine addicts them to it. She found that smoking causes many illnesses, leads to a shorter life for many, and raises medical costs for everyone. The most vulnerable, she learned, are young people like her friends and herself. With productive activities already in mind, Ireni organized the information she gathered into what she called her Smoking Package.

Productivity: Fired up by her findings and concerned about her friends and family, Ireni decided to mount a no-smoking campaign. She invited others to join her and started with a committee of three people. They produced a pamphlet to hand out, organized a No-Smoking Rally, and sponsored a No-Smoking Day. As they progressed, others joined. The small rally for her grade featured a talk by her friend's dad (the doctor) and sign-up sheets both for promising not to start smoking and for promising to quit if you already smoked. The No-Smoking Day picked up when the girls challenged the boys to stop for a week. Ireni decided not to smoke.

• • •

In these three ways of learning—experience, study, and productivity—students are learning more than content and process. They are also learning how to become positive, active people and how to work successfully with others (see Table 4.1). The structure of SDL in general, and learning episodes in particular, is designed for development in both the personal and social domains and offers many opportunities for teaching in them. The focus on inner direction, challenge, and self-reliance, for example, regularly involves personal issues. Similarly, the transitional teaching strategy—from class to group to personal activities—in addition to activities in teams and the use of advisory and support groups, provides regular opportunities for dealing with social skills. Students learn on their own, from each other, and during instruction; at the same time, they learn about themselves, working with others, and how to learn from instruction. Taken together, these aspects integrate the fundamental elements of learning into a powerful unit.

Chapter 5

Teaching Independent Thinking

SKILLS are the basic units of SDL activity. They are the means by which students learn to experience the world, investigate it, and get things done in it. There is no end to skills. We are always learning new ones, and the supply is inexhaustible. Here, we focus on a few basic SDL skills and how to teach them and then examine a process that students can use to develop skills on their own. The intention is to build a repertoire of skills and add to it regularly.

Skills and processes are the portable instruments of SDL that enable us to learn in a variety of situations and to accomplish whatever we choose. They are portable because we can employ each of them in many different activities and situations. Like riding our fabled bicycle, once we know how to do it, we seldom lose the touch. These learning skills are important for another reason: skills create competence, and competence is power, the power to get things done. The competent enjoy the pleasures of activity beyond the obvious, below the surface of things. They also enjoy the rewards that are available to those capable of predictable success. The very competent enjoy what Mihaly Csikszentmihalyi (1990) refers to as "flow," the elation of total absorption.

Skills are joined to create processes, which are procedures for accomplishing complex tasks. The process of investigation, for example, is an orderly step-by-step sequence of skillful acts that begins with a question and leads to an answer. We will examine several processes, and all are valuable, but no list of processes will prepare students for every situation. The best preparation for using processes is learning process thinking, that is, learning to ask, when confronted by a task to accomplish, "What is the best procedure for me to follow? What sequence of steps must I follow to get this job done efficiently and well?" Process thinking involves standing back, imagining the job completed, and then working backward to identify the steps required to get there.

Skills can be clustered into groups and then organized into processes for accomplishing certain kinds of tasks. A cluster on action learning, for example, would include such skills as goal setting, planning the activities, organizing resources, taking action, problem solving, and assessing progress and success. These are the basic skills of action learning and the basic headings in the action learning proposals that students develop. A student in Colorado created the opportunity to map underground caves [*goal*]. He developed a program of underground experiences, studies in cave mapping, and actual mapping activities [*plan*]. He negotiated time in the caves, organized the equipment he needed, and drew up a schedule of activities [*organization*]. After initiating his plan [*taking action*], he ran into several obstacles that had to be addressed and overcome [*problem solving*]. Finally, he listed the evidence and criteria that would demonstrate a successful result [*assessment*].

Skills can also be organized into processes around such themes as investigation, creativity, communication, and reflection. Investigation involves skills in observation, establishing a key question, gathering evidence, analyzing evidence, and drawing conclusions from it. For example, as a result of observing the September 11, 2001, catastrophe, a student in New York City decided to investigate Islam, specifically the relationship between the Koran and terrorism. The question was, "What is the justification in Islam for terrorist acts?" She gathered evidence from interviews, reading, and the Internet, then drew her conclusions, made her argument, and prepared her presentation. Each step was a new and challenging skill, just as it is in other clusters.

Creativity involves the capacity for generating original ideas and the skill for producing works from them in every field from painting to architecture. Communication involves sending and receiving clear and effective messages. If communication is interaction with others, reflection is communication and interaction with oneself. Both groups of skills are essential for success in SDL.

By exercising skills and processes, students master competencies, which they can apply to academics and any other form of learning and accomplishment. (See Resource F for examples of process templates.)

Inviting Inquiry and Initiative

To be successful in SDL, students have to learn to think for themselves. Thinking independently is the first of the four stages in moving from TDL to SDL; it is the foundation on which the other stages stand. David Reisman's lonely crowd (1950) waits to be told what to think, what to feel, and what to do. They have been controlled and directed for so long that they have no inner direction. They do not know who to turn to or what to do. In SDL, we teach students to be inner directed rather than "other directed." That process begins by teaching them to think, decide, form opinions, make choices, and take action—informed, passionate action (see Exhibit 5.1). The flying model is a good one: the student experiences flight, goes to ground school to complete the required studies, and then one day pilots a plane. It is a classic learning episode in which the student's experience leads to study and the study to action.

TDL does not usually emphasize independent, individual, self-directed thinking. It depends too much on teacher direction and telling in order to get through the content. Independent thinking depends on asking, and not just asking any question, but asking key questions worth answering. We can begin by thinking of course outcomes as questions: "What is geometry designed to do?" "Why did men in the Civil War stand and walk toward each other across open ground while firing?" "Why does the earth not fall out of the solar system into space?" The question should be about an important issue worth knowing and should provoke student interest.

Wiggins and McTeghe (1998) recommend converting a course to essential questions and then deriving unit questions from them. One way to derive essential questions is to look through the textbook or other references

---

EXHIBIT 5.1

How Teachers Encourage Students to Think

Teachers encourage students to think when . . .
- They ask more than they tell.
- They pose challenging but answerable questions.
- They ask students to give their opinions and to support them.
- They never embarrass students about their answers.
- They ask students to take a position based on evidence.
- They ask other students to extend the thinking one student offers.
- They create a comfortable "in this together" atmosphere.
- They give students problems to solve in teams first, then as individuals.
- They lead a discussion of the question as a moderator until a conclusion is reached.
- They pursue the question with students by establishing hypotheses and testing them to find defensible answers.
- They hold debates and trials and run case studies.
- They challenge students to challenge themselves with provocative questions to pursue.
- They equip students with a repertoire of questioning and answering strategies.

and determine the major questions the content answers. A chapter on adaptation in a biology text, for example, may suggest the essential question, "How does an organism's structure enable it to survive in its environment?" If essential questions are too broad for presentation by themselves, more focused unit questions can be derived from them, such as, "How do the structures of amphibians and reptiles support their survival?" These questions launch investigations that lead to a thorough understanding of the issues involved. Wiggins and McTeghe note that thorough understanding is achieved when students can explain concepts clearly with supporting evidence, interpret major ideas in accurate translations of them, apply what they learn in new contexts, gain perspective by seeing different points of view and the relationship of knowledge to a larger framework of ideas, empathize with thoughts and attitudes different from their own, and gain the self-knowledge to understand both their own ways of thinking and what is necessary to comprehend at an even deeper level.

The spirit of inquiry should also lead regularly to investigations conducted as a class. That inquiry will lead directly to the search for relevant information, which may come from a variety of sources. In one middle school class, the teacher asked, "Where are you from?" She meant several generations back. The students' search was conducted primarily through interviews with relatives. Students reported on their findings, discussed and demonstrated what life was like in those former homelands, and then with a line of wool traced their families' journey on a map of the world. By the end, the world was crisscrossed with lines, and the picture had become the class's personal symbol.

Questions can also be the framework for a schoolwide curriculum. The faculty at Francis W. Parker Charter Essential School in Devens, Massachusetts, developed an inquiry-based curriculum. Each year an essential question is addressed schoolwide—for example, "What is community?" "What is change?" and "What really matters?" This essential question generates subquestions, for example, "What is a function?" "Is light a particle or a wave?" "What is good writing?" "How is society reflected in culture?" and "Who are you?" These questions are addressed through action learning activities, such as class investigations, group projects, and individual research. The subject areas are integrated into three domains of study. Students progress through three divisions, roughly equal to two grades each, by making gateway presentations to a committee in which they make their cases for advancement, exhibit their portfolios, and answer questions. One of several requirements for graduation is a senior project based on the student's own essential question, such as these proposed by recent seniors: "What components make an air conditioner?" "What makes the news?"

"How did we get here?" and "What are the effects of outdoor education on adolescent girls?" The required ingredients in the senior project are an interdisciplinary approach, a research component, academic rigor, collaboration with people outside the school community, and benefit from the student's work to the larger community. It is a design for teaching students to think and act independently.

To think for themselves, students need a repertoire of skills, and the first skill is the ability to ferret out the information they need to answer their questions. Searching for information can take a number of forms. Students should be skilled in using print and Internet resources, but they should also learn to find information as directly as possible through fieldwork, interviews, and contact with others through the Web. Gathering information includes making sense of it. Students should learn to examine information carefully and make sense of it well enough to explain it.

The jigsaw group activity is an excellent technique that requires each member to explain a body of information clearly enough to teach it to the others. In a study of life in the twelfth century, for example, the class is divided into groups, and each member of the group is given a role as a different kind of medieval person: a peasant, a nobleman, a knight, a priest, a country woman, and a child. The group then disperses, with each person going to a group that contains students from other groups with the same role. Together they study the role they chose or were assigned. All the priests, for instance, meet to study and discuss the materials provided. When they are prepared, the original groups reconvene and each member explains his or her life in the twelfth century. They each hold a piece of the jigsaw puzzle and contribute to the whole.

An important part of learning to think independently is being able to stand back and see the larger picture. In this way, students learn perspective, the relative importance of things, and how forces interplay to create dynamic situations. This kind of systems view lends itself to graphics that show the major subsystems of a situation and how the subsystems interact with each other to create force fields of influence. The chart of terrorism, for example, would span the map. A model of each form of terror would show its origin, method, and motive. Soon we can see links among some and the isolation of others. Analysis shows the interconnections among blocks of information, enabling us to understand the larger issues and more significant questions. Dealing with key issues makes learning alive and real for students rather than remote, abstract, and irrelevant.

Another important aspect of thinking for oneself is making decisions and solving problems. When we are told and controlled, we have few decisions to make or problems to solve. Yet life is a steady stream of decisions and crises. How our life flows depends on the quality of the decisions we make and our ingenuity and determination at solving the problems that impede us. To learn to make decisions, we first need decisions to make. SDL provides them. Teachers help students to identify when a decision is called for. They need to know that there are always choices. Everything we do is the result of a choice we have, and choices have consequences. Teach students to list the alternatives along with the advantages and disadvantages of each one, to weigh the choices and make an informed decision. At some point, choices deserve a values discussion, that is, a conversation based on the fact that each choice we make reflects our values. That could lead to a discussion of what values are and which of them are worth holding and living by.

People who think for themselves have opinions, take positions, and work out platforms on which their actions will be based. This means analyzing the situation, examining the evidence, and determining one's answer to the question at hand. Suppose that question is, "Why do the seasons change?" We gather the evidence, then organize our reasoning, and decide on the answer we will present. Taking and defending a position is rehearsed in such activities as debates, trials, case studies, and dramatizations.

Exhibit 5.2 is an example of a trial for World War II leaders that makes students think. The teacher who developed it, Keith Butler at Oak Bay High School in Victoria, British Columbia, teaches his students to think independently by punctuating his modern history course with a series of jury trials on such issues as the atomic bombing of Hiroshima, Josef Stalin's methods of shaping the Soviet Union into a superpower, intervention in the Vietnam War, and Neville Chamberlain's policy of appeasement in World War II. The trial featured in Exhibit 5.2 asks the jury to decide whether Otto Ohlendorf, the commander of Einstazgruppen D, should be held responsible for crimes against humanity. In World War II, the Einstazgruppen followed the German army to exterminate so-called undesirables from newly occupied territory. Several commanders, including Ohlendorf, later became directors of concentration camps.

These are calm descriptions of features in a dynamic class of curious investigators and skilled entrepreneurial performers. Such features of learning to think independently arise because SDL requires them and allows for them. They are the thinking skills that productive people need. Here is a summary of the thinking skills discussed in this chapter:

- Ask questions: Inquire into the nature of things.

- Find relevant information: Conduct an investigation to find information.

- Analyze the situation: Place the issue in perspective. Stand back and see the larger picture.

EXHIBIT 5.2

A Jury Trial Approach to Thinking Independently

Keith Butler teaches his students to think independently by punctuating his Modern History course with a series of jury trials on such key issues as the atomic bombing of Hiroshima, Joseph Stalin's methods of shaping the Soviet Union into a superpower, intervention in the Vietnam War, and Neville Chamberlain's policy of appeasement in World War II.

Trial No. 3 reads, "The jury will be asked to decide whether Otto Ohlendorf, Commander of Einstazgruppen D, should be held responsible for 'crimes against humanity.'" In World War II, the Einstazgruppen followed the German Army to eliminate so-called "undesirables" from newly occupied territory. Several commanders, including Ohlendorf, later became directors of concentration camps.

Roles
- Lawyers: Two prosecutors, two defense lawyers
- Witnesses: Hitler, Himmler, and Hess
- Jury: All remaining class members

Lawyers

Lawyers prepare by reading the text and an evidence package and then follow a five-step guide:

1. Prepare a pretrial brief; include your arguments.
2. Predict the other side's arguments; prepare your responses.
3. Choose three witnesses; frame your questions. Research the other side's witnesses; frame your questions.
4. Prepare opening and closing statements.
5. Gather evidence and exhibits in a trial book to support arguments.

Lawyers are required to present their witnesses with a trial brief two weeks before the trial date.

Witnesses

Witnesses are responsible for researching their characters. They follow three steps:

1. Research your character; prepare a time line; relate your character to the trial.
2. Meet with your lawyer to review questions and answers.
3. Predict the opposing lawyers' questions; develop answers.

Jury

Each jury member completes a juror worksheet and after the trial writes a one- to two-page juror report summarizing the trial and judging the weight of the evidence.

Note: Emily Shelton was one of the defending lawyers on the Ohlendorf case who won an unpopular acquittal for the client.

Source: *Outlined with permission from Keith Butler, Oak Bay High School, Victoria, British Columbia.*

- Make thoughtful decisions: Weigh the alternatives, and make a thoughtful choice.

- Formulate a position: Consider the evidence, decide on your answer or position, and defend it with evidence and reason.

- Test the truth of your position: Conduct a test or experiment to see if the position you have taken proves to be the right one.

- Decide what should be done: Determine the action to take to express your thinking on the issue.

- Solve problems that arise: Address your problems, consider alternatives, choose the best, and act on it.

Developing Problem-Solving Skills

Students should learn to test the truth of the positions they adopt and of those they have adopted in the past. They are constantly building their own knowledge system and the perspectives on the world that will guide their lives. It is important that they be examined. As Socrates said, "The unexamined life is not worth living" or can easily be lived badly. And it is important to examine our actions, because as Aristotle said, "We are what we are doing." The examination can be philosophical (related to values and character) or scientific (related to facts and proofs). A scientific style of investigation begins by stating the proposition as a hypothesis and then developing a test that convincingly proves or disproves its validity. Teachers might ask, for example, "What are the causes of bullying?" After examining many possibilities, the class may decide that bullies have low self-esteem. The challenge is to find a way to test a hypothesis and then to measure opinions against the evidence.

One aspect of thinking independently that often gets lost or crushed in the rush of coverage and testing knowledge is students' generation of their own original ideas, thoughts, and creative products. Stimulating generativity is essential to SDL. Opportunities should be offered and creativity and originality invited as often as possible. Teachers should let it be known that creative alternatives to assignments and packages are always welcome. Offering time and stimulating experiences helps, but the best stimulant is spending sustained time on a topic or field of activity. Reaching a depth of understanding and active work with concepts nurture new ideas. Learning such practices as metaphorical thinking, diagramming, and brainstorming can stimulate generativity.

In SDL, it soon becomes time to take action, to decide what one wants to do or should do, to determine what is important. We do not encourage much reflection in schools; perhaps that is because there is little provocation to stimulate it. But in SDL, there are many decisions to make that will have strong influences on the students' studies and their lives. They must turn inward and reflect. Contemplation, or more simply, inner dialogue, is an essential skill. It is the inward version of the outward debate, except that it is with oneself, a dialogue in which possibilities are raised and weighed and decisions are made.

Once students decide and take action, they soon begin confronting problems. Problems are serious impediments. Students are not used to confronting them and are as likely to drop the activity as struggle to overcome them. But SDL requires determined effort, ingenious strategy, and great pride in being unstoppable. (See Resource G for encouragement in the face of obstacles.)

Exhibit 5.3 outlines one problem-solving strategy to teach to students. The trap lies in quitting at the first sign of difficulty rather than systematically searching for a solution. Solutions require a sense of self-efficacy based on a few successes and well-earned feedback about them. Cultivate pride in students who are determined to overcome obstacles in their path. Be overwhelmed with excitement when they do.

Using Process Frameworks: Investigation and Action

Processes are the patterns that we follow in order to get things done. I refer to outlines of processes that can be applied to many situations as templates. Once we recognize the task and situation, we select the appropriate process

---

EXHIBIT 5.3

The Creative Problem Solver

Projects that we manage ourselves seldom run as smoothly as projects that are looked after by others. When problems arise, we are challenged to solve them ourselves rather than give up—the easy response. Be confident that you can solve your own problems; be proud when you do. Develop an attitude. And when you have tried everything, you can still ask for help. Here is one approach that works:

1. *State the problem clearly and exactly.* Once you think clearly about what the real problem is, the solution will be easier. Often, the real problem is that we are thinking fuzzy or avoiding thinking about the problem at all. Get to the core of it.
2. *Study the problem.* List everything you know about the problem. Understand it. Is there something else you need to know or discover? Often, the solution is difficult because we do not know enough about the problem itself.
3. *Brainstorm a solution to the problem.* List as many ways as possible for solving the problem. Be creative, imaginative, and daring. Visualize. Stick with it. Develop several alternatives.
4. *Select the best solution.* Pick the two or three best solutions, and then decide which of them you will use. Think each through. Imagine yourself using the solution, and visualize what will likely happen.
5. *Develop the solution for action.* Outline step by step what you will do to make the chosen solution work.
6. *Just do it.* The weak and helpless practice being weak and helpless every day. The strong and successful daily practice overcoming the difficulties that stand in their way.

template and apply it. With a repertoire of process templates available to us, we can take the next step to process thinking. Faced with any task, we think it through carefully, deciding on the steps in a process that will enable us to complete the task successfully and efficiently.

Exhibit 5.4 is an investigative process template. Process templates for four other important learning processes are outlined in Resource F, and, of course, others can be prepared. In addition, the outlines can be sharpened or extended and are critical for a life of learning. Each template also says, "This kind of learning is important." The investigation template in Exhibit 5.4, for instance, not only says, "Here is how to investigate a question or issue." It also says, "You should have questions that you want to investigate."

Each template is a process that can be applied to many different learning activities in different fields or subjects. When students develop a repertoire of templates that they can apply on their own, they are learning how to learn, a major goal of education. And when they put the templates together, they are learning how to pursue excellence in a field of activity. Here is what one SDL teacher had to say about this kind of teaching:

> Let me put it bluntly. I'm not going to teach my students anything that's not interesting, important, or useful, no matter how many tests it's going to be on. Teaching that stuff puts my kids on the intellectual rock pile, and they aren't guilty.

The individual steps in each process are skills or subprocesses that need to be elaborated, taught, and practiced. Templates are not only patterns of learning processes; they are also frameworks for teaching related skills. They are skill clusters or sequences that work together to produce a single kind of achievement.

EXHIBIT 5.4

Investigation Template

The informed mind is a watershed for purposeful thought and action.

Explore areas of interest and concern.	Find a key issue.
Raise questions.	Find and frame key question.
Consider possible sources.	Choose and pursue sources.
Collect information.	Organize information.
Form an answer, position, or hypothesis.	Gather and review supporting evidence.
Test against reality and counterarguments.	Present and defend your position.

Examples: Answering any question, such as What is the best kind of car to buy? What caused the Iraqi-Allied coalition war? Conducting any scientific or other formal investigation.

Students can use the templates in many situations in school, at work, and at home for the rest of their lives. Even more important than using these templates is the gradual inculcation of process thinking. Faced with a task, we want students to think process naturally: "What procedure can I follow to get this job done successfully and swiftly?" "What step-by-step process provides a direct, efficient pathway to the outcome I'm after?" Using the process templates provides an introduction to such process thinking.

The template outlines are designed as if students are using them in open-ended or lifelike situations. If a teacher is introducing them within a course or subject, the beginning steps in the outline may be different. Templates can also be employed as challenges. Students can be challenged to conduct an important investigation, seek a key experience, or develop proposals for the pursuit of all of the templates. These can also be introduced at appropriate times during the year as students learn to become excellent in the fields they choose.

In a unit on the nature of human conflict, for example, the question may arise, "Why did the United States and the coalition go to war with Iraq?" This question gives the teacher the key issue of the investigation template. Together, teacher and students can raise related questions and then focus on the key question to answer, which could be, "What motivated Iraq to invade Kuwait, and what motivated the United States and the coalition forces to conduct a war against Iraq in the wake of that invasion?" Finding the key question and stating it clearly is the rock on which the process rests.

Next comes considering sources from which information related to the question can be gathered. Suggestions of such sources can be taken from students and listed and rated for the reliability of the information they would yield. A neighbor's opinion, for example, would normally rate lower than the *New York Times*, but even information from the *New York Times* has limitations. What about Iraqi and independent points of view? Note that the search is not for someone else's answer but for the information from which to shape one's own answer. In this way, students identify and pursue useful sources, perhaps in teams. They search out information, and then collect and organize it according to a strategy that sorts out the information into useful categories. In the example, perhaps the categories will be the U.S., Iraqi, and independent points of view.

With the information thus arrayed, one or more hypotheses or proposed answers are raised and then supported as thoroughly as possible with arguments from the evidence. Counterarguments are tried. The students examine the record to see if the proposed answer stands the test of reality and common sense. If the answer survives, it is accepted, but tentatively, because new information or insights may change it.

In the example, the teacher introduced the investigation template by acting like a commander-in-chief working with her staff of students to form a position about the Iraq-Kuwait conflict. It was an excellent choice because it was so laden with conditions capable of distorting the truth. These same conditions also suggest caution, which is often part of true investigations. In this case, the class broke into three teams, each taking a different point of view: coalition, Iraqi, and independent. As they collected information, they held brief cross-position confrontations. Each prepared a situation report. From these, the class developed a three-team time line of Middle East events over the past fifty years and mapped the situation at five critical periods. Each team used these visuals as props in their debate of the proposition (intentionally set as counter to reality) that Iraq had a right to invade and the coalition no right to interfere.

Following the debate, the students wrestled with their own personal positions on the issue and how they would present their arguments convincingly to a panel concerned with only one thing: proving it. They tried out their arguments on their support teams and then revised and tried again. Finally, they presented their arguments either orally or in writing, and the panel, which in this case included the teacher, judged the degree to which each applicant's case was made. As a final act, the commander-in-chief reviewed the process with her staff of students. They underlined their successes and identified ways to improve the next time they conducted an investigation.

The teacher's role here is to monitor students and coach them as they apply the templates to their own individual work. This supervision is enhanced if students use the template headings in their journals and in their submitted work, at least until the process is habitual for them. The template approach is also a way of thinking. Students should be encouraged to sketch out a template for any activity that involves time and energy. Framing activities is the strategic approach to learning and doing.

Cultivating Process Thinking and Attitudes

Students of SDL have a great deal to learn. They must absorb the prescribed curriculum for a course. They learn how to go about learning it independently. They also need to learn how to plan their own curriculum, whether it is a project, a unit, a course, or program. And they have to learn how to achieve their own learning goals in the most effective possible style.

Essential Skills

Once students set out to learn on their own, several skills become essential:

• *Students have to learn how to decide exactly what they are going to learn.* In some cases, this will require deciding what they need to learn, and in others it will mean determining what they most want to learn. If the need is to learn the curriculum, everything should be done to find a relationship between the subject and the students' own concerns and experience. If the situation is what they most want to learn, students should be helped to discover interests, strengths, and revealing experiences. Whether need or interest, the result should be a clearly stated outcome that the student values. These goal statements will communicate the student's intentions to everyone involved and will act as both a guide and a commitment to the work of the student. It is the single most important component of an SDL activity.

• *Students have to devise a plan.* The plan will be a sequence of learning strategies or activities that the student chooses and organizes as "the best way to get to the goal that I can devise." Students learn to be guided by the demands of the situation and their own learning strengths and preferences in selecting their learning activities.

• *Students have to manage their own time, effort, and resources, even when the activities are assigned.* One way is to teach students to create an action timetable. They begin with an overall record of all of their project activities and the date when each will be completed. Learning to predict how long activities will take, monitor how long they do take, and adapt so that the project is completed on time are essential skills. Managing effort, achieving self-motivation, and developing self-discipline are the major challenges of SDL for many students.

• *Students have to keep a record of their experience.* This should be a record of events, but also a critical commentary on them. Students should be required to comment on the success of all of their choices, strategies, and efforts. Successes need to be acknowledged, but difficulties should be noted, analyzed, and remedied. No matter what the activity is—study, practice, planning, or taking action—analyzing and regulating performance is a key source of learning to learn efficiently and successfully.

This planning process raises two other essential skills and practices: becoming inner directed and learning how to interact with others. Becoming inner directed means becoming directed by one's own thoughts and feelings. Many aspects of the action process require students to turn inward, weigh possibilities, and make decisions. This freedom is possible only if students can control and manage their own attitudes and behavior. Finding interests and developing passions require students to understand themselves to the core of their basic desires and interests. Self-motivation involves an ongoing inner dialogue to establish and reinforce an entrepreneurial perspective—pursuit with high energy—combined with an optimistic expectation of success at what is begun. Moving away from the easy and familiar and engaging in risky and challenging activities all require inner strength: courage, determination, and confidence. And what we hope for our students is deep involvement in a field—complete absorption in a compelling activity at a high level of skill. When the course is over, we want them to feel pride in what they have accomplished and who they have become. Becoming self-directed usually involves transformation, that is, a change in attitude, perspective, and behavior. Student reports and testimonies often center on struggle and emergence. It is an elixir for both the student and the teacher.

For these reasons, it is important to focus on helping students to become more self-aware. Help them to clarify their own thoughts and feelings and understand their strengths and how to apply them. It is also important to teach them to exercise self-control and self-management. They need to be trustworthy and cooperative, as well as assertive and daring. And they need to be skillful at managing themselves. Self-direction depends on a set of attitudes that must be developed. Chief among them are clarity of purpose, the confidence to plan, the courage to act, openness to feedback, the determination to overcome difficulties, and the reflective ability to draw learning from experience and apply it to future plans. (See Resource E for more on this topic.)

SDL is an individual activity, but it is far from solitary. Students learn from other students and adults, work together on learning activities and projects, help each other to achieve their goals, and learn together how to learn on their own. Life is largely a social activity, and so is much of learning. For these reasons, it is important for students to learn how to relate to others, participate productively in a group, communicate positively, and understand how to fix the way a group is operating when the work is not going well. These, too, are life skills as well as SDL course skills. The small group is a crucible of learning.

Personal and Social Issues

Personal and social issues arise from the beginning of an SDL course as teachers require students to take initiative and participate actively. Connect students to their past successes as models, and relate activities to their current concerns. Introduce them to the concept of the hero's journey—the story of initiative, struggle, and transformation. Teach them the inner work as you teach them to plan and act. Teach them how to function as a group, teach them social skills through game activities, and teach them to troubleshoot problems that arise in group work.

In SDL, students learn how to learn what they have to learn, and they learn how to plan and negotiate what they choose to learn. Success in those activities, as in the rest of life, involves self-awareness and the ability to work with and learn from others. These are skills that can be learned and taught.

Expressing Skills and Processes as Competencies

Important skills and processes can be expressed as competencies and assigned as outcomes that require students to make themselves proficient in applying them. A biology teacher, for example, may require students to demonstrate their ability to observe acutely by studying a plant species in the field and describing its features, functioning, and relationships in as much detail as possible. This approach places the responsibility on students to develop the skill and apply it in some challenging way as a demonstration of their success. A complete course can be assigned as such competencies. With the responsibility for learning clearly defined, the teacher can then focus on providing what students need to achieve their goals.

Students learn to apply their skills in the contracts that they write and the projects they pursue. The emphasis on taking action with consequences makes successful execution important. Action also provides realistic skill practice, and success provides the reward.

When taking action is the focus, learning to think in terms of processes and systems becomes important. Process thinking is looking at the task to be done and seeing the most efficient or appropriate path to completing it. Systems thinking is becoming aware of the dynamic interaction of forces in which the process is embedded. If a student decides to build a laboratory or clubhouse, for example, his first task is to lay out an efficient process that would involve such steps as designing it, gathering the materials and tools required, and developing a sequence for the actual construction. The process is critical, but if the system of dynamics that impinge on it is not also studied, disaster can easily strike. The system, in this case, may include the response of parents, the attitudes of neighbors, and the local ordinances that govern construction and public safety. Students are empowered to act when they learn to seek out the most practical and effective way—the best process—for getting the job done and when they can analyze the pattern of influences—the system—that must be dealt with to make the process workable.

These are ways of thinking that can be learned and perfected through practice. Teach students to stop for reflection before they rush into action. Teach them to think through the process—the step-by-step procedure they must follow to get from where they are to where they want to be. Have them list the things that must be done, and then find the best possible procedure for doing them. There are laborious and boring processes and efficient and elegant ones. Teachers can design basic templates for processes that students can follow to guide them through often-repeated activities (see Resource F for examples of process templates), but elegant processes are designed by students to suit their tasks and to accommodate their preferences and strengths.

Process thinking is the basic skill required for successful planning. Systems thinking is very useful for anticipating problems and for solving them. For success in SDL, think skills, processes, and systems.

• • •

All of the elements examined in this chapter are applied when students develop their plans for self-directed activities. Learning agreements, the topic of the next chapter, require the application of skills and processes. Teachers can also help students to see how their choices of activities are embedded in the larger systems that have an impact on their lives.

Chapter 6

Negotiating Student Learning Agreements

WHEN STUDENTS are preparing to launch their individual activities, they usually write up a proposal to present to their teachers and others for consideration. They may be proposing a personal approach to achieving a course outcome or competency; it may be a week-, month-, or year-long project, or it may be a major challenge or passage that they will work on throughout grades 11 and 12. The contract is a form that students follow when outlining their proposals for the self-directed learning activities that they have decided to pursue. It usually includes a formal declaration of what the student proposes to do, why that activity is important, how they intend to accomplish it, and the criteria by which they will assess their achievement. By the time students write up contracts, their ideas have usually been reviewed and discussed in their advisory groups and support triads, groups of three students each who help each other with their SDL activities (see Resource H). Students submit their contracts and negotiate the final design of their activities with their teachers.

The Learning Agreement or Contract

The formal agreement or contract is a valuable multipurpose instrument. As a form, it outlines the basic elements of the SDL process and guides students through the steps that they have to consider. It becomes an agenda for student-teacher meetings to negotiate the final form of this learning agreement and a detailed record of what both parties proposed and agreed to. As such, it will be referred to many times and may become the basis for renegotiation later, if circumstances require it. When both parties, and perhaps others, sign the proposal, it takes on the weight of a contract and signals to the student the commitment that has been made. The contract outlines a process of strategic action learning that students will use for the rest of their lives.

The contract can take many forms. Teachers should consider all of the possible elements and then design their own. The core of the outline is the goal, outcome, or competency that the student decides to pursue, and the plan devised to accomplish it. Here is a simple example:

Goal: To figure out the stats for Hal Ripken in the last ten games of his baseball career

Plan:

- Watch some games; read reports on the others.
- Keep a record of at-bats and performance (at the plate and in the field).
- Figure out the statistics.
- Compare Ripken's performance to that of other third basemen.
- Write a report.

The Elements of a Contract

The student begins by preparing a contract that addresses the major elements in the planning process. A full sample contract is shown in Exhibit 6.1.

EXHIBIT 6.1

Negotiated Learning Contract

Student ___Adrian Boyes___   Parent or Sponsor ___Al Boyes___   Teacher ___Mrs. Dent___

1. GOAL: What concrete, specific achievement can you pursue within the time available that is an important step toward your vision? Challenge yourself. State your goal clearly so that you and others will know when you reach it.

   I want to learn to read at grade 10 level.

2. IMPORTANCE: Why is this goal important to you? What is the picture in your mind of how you would most like to be different a year from now? What will you be like and be doing? What will you know and be good at? Where will you be and with whom? Where are you headed? Toward what wonderful vision of excellence?

   I'm failing English 10 because I can't read Julius Caesar and I need it to pass because I dropped other courses. If you can't read everything is hard. I don't want to repeat grade 10.

EXHIBIT 6.1 (continued)

3. PLAN: A detailed, step-by-step plan of exactly what you will do to achieve your goal, or a list of the experiences, studies, and productive activities you will use in your plan.

A. Experiences: A list of experiences that would help you on your quest.

   · *Mary Ellen reads a lot and real fast. She might show me how she does it.*
   · *I could read the sports pages and talk to jocks.*

B. Studies: An outline of what you need to know and how you will find out about it and learn it.

   · *I don't really know how to read. The tricks. I need someone to show me how. (I'm slow. Word attack skills grade 8.4.)*
   · *Practice my skills. Maybe in a workbook or something.*
   · *Check the Internet and library for programs.*

C. Productive Activities: An outline of the activities you will pursue and the skills you need to do them well.

   · *Read more books*
   · *My granddad and me are going to read To Kill a Mockingbird and talk about it and see the video.*
   · *My aunt is sick. I'll read to her.*

4. CHALLENGE: Action plans are often preparation for a challenging activity in which you risk new behavior in a task that tests and demonstrates your new achievements. Describe your challenge here.

   I will read Julius Caesar by Shakespeare

5. PROBLEM SOLVING: Difficulties will arise. They can be avoided by anticipation and preparation.

A. Anticipated Difficulties: List things that could make progress difficult: your shortcomings and mistakes, problems with others, technical problems, and so on.

   I don't study much or read so that's going to be my big problem.

B. Proposed Solutions: Answer each difficulty with a strategy of what you can do to make sure it does not stop your progress.

   I'll have to start studying and read and keep at it some how.

(continued)

EXHIBIT 6.1 (continued)

6. MANAGEMENT: Organize yourself for efficiency and success. Find a place to work, gather resources you need, plan how you will spend your time, and begin. Take charge of your time and your life.

- Resources Needed: List your material, human, and technical needs—the supplies, people, and equipment you need to do your work. Figure out where and how to get them.

  - *People to Contact: Mary Ellen, a reading tutor, granddad, Aunt Judith*
  - *Resources: I need a card from the public library, a computer, and a video player (Granddad's?) I need a reading workbook, an internet or video program, or exercises to practice.*
  - *Places: I need a place to sit and read and study. A desk in my room.*

- Timetable: Make a calendar of dates. Detail what parts of your plan will be completed on those days. Divide your activity into two or three phases to use as check points with your support team.

  My plan is just for the first week, then we'll see. All the time—read 30 min. a day.
  - *Make all my phone calls.*
  - *Arrange with counsellor for a tutor or reading teacher.*
  - *Library—card and books.*
  - *Read to Aunt Judith on Tuesdays after BB practice*
  - *Talk to Granddad on Thursday nights*
  - *Set up some kind of reading practice (with tutor)*

7. EVALUATION: Establish a framework now that will enable you to judge later how much you did and how well. Your challenge is always to improve as much as possible on where you are now. Be able to show others.

Baseline Measure: A clear demonstration of how much you know and how well you can perform in this activity now—the base against which your progress will be measured.

  They gave me a test. My scores are my baseline. Word attack grade 8.2. Decoding 8.6. Speed 80 wpm. Comprehension 9.4. Vocabulary 12.6

8. PROGRESS MEASURE: Describe these levels of improvement in observable terms others can confirm.

Minimum progress (smallest acceptable improvement)

  I raise my low scores a grade level. I read one book.

EXHIBIT 6.1 (continued)

Satisfactory progress (basic competence, average improvement)

I raise my scores two grade levels. I read two books.

Excellent progress (significant improvement, outstanding achievement)

I raise my scores to grade 10 or higher. I read three or more books, including Julius C.

9. DEMONSTRATION: How will you demonstrate to yourself and others what you have learned and achieved? As always, choose the best way.

I will show my scores before and after. I will read a part of one of my books I think is good to the class and tell why. You told me I should also talk about what I learned.

10. CELEBRATION: What is the most appropriate, rewarding, and pleasurable way you can celebrate what you achieve in this activity?

If I make it to grade 10 reading I would like to get something that says what I did and I can show at home. A party would be good with those big sundaes and cherries and bananas.

Source: *Reproduced with permission from Personal Power Press International, Inc.*

Adrian will be exciting to teach; he recognizes his shortcomings, he is eager to correct them, and he has some good ideas. His student-teacher conference should be a great one. The contract he used represents one of many possible levels of complexity and many different kinds of learning agreement.

Teachers can begin simply with a goal and a plan, or they can create planning booklets of ideas, drafts, learning plans, reports, and reflections. The agreement is an outline of the SDL process. Create the design that best suits you, your students, and your situation; that's what SDL teachers do.

Goal or Outcome

The most important group of headings in the contract is about the specific project that the student is proposing and a statement of the goal or outcome that the student seeks. The outcome may be a competency to achieve or a task to accomplish. If it is simply a course outcome everyone has to achieve, this statement will make the student's personal approach clear. A requirement to understand wave action, for example, may lead to such goals as "to teach wave action to a class of sixth graders," "to build a wave tank with my group and study wave action," "to describe the perfect surfing wave scientifically," or "to complete packages 7 and 8 on wave action." A major project or passage will involve a broader and more personal outcome, such as "to study biology research and ethics," "to apply chaos theory to individual lifelines," "to become skilled at navigation using instruments," or "to study the osprey and find ways to preserve the species."

The contract, like SDL activities in general, relates to the goal statement. The statement is critical and should be precise, but it is also problematical. Goals are set with limited knowledge about them and what is involved in achieving them. The reality may be very different from what the student imagined in conceiving it. Goals may turn out to be too difficult to achieve, and circumstances may make pursuing them impossible. Or students may get bored or come to despise the goals they chose. Minimize these dangers by encouraging students to do an exploratory probe into the activity first and to make a realistic estimate of the time and effort required for completion.

Be prepared to renegotiate contracts to correct the errors of judgment that led to them, but not to avoid the difficulties involved in achieving any worthy goal. It may also help to employ what one teacher calls "pathway planning," which means planning the first few steps and then, from that experience, planning what the next few steps should be. Making every goal as rich as possible by building into it many valuable related goals makes completion more likely. Making the wave tank, for example, becomes a rich goal if the student wishes to learn to make a water tank, solve the problem of ship stability in strong seas, talk with his father (who is in the navy) about it, or work with a team of peers on the project—especially if it is for a competition. And if this student is thinking about a career in hydrology or hydromechanics, as well as completing the project for physics class, the goal becomes an even more powerful guide.

Importance

When they fill out this section of the contract, students think about the task they have selected and write an explanation of why they chose it. The teacher often focuses on this statement in the process of negotiating the contract with the student to ensure that the goal is carefully chosen and for good reasons. Some of the concerns about goal selection are as follows:

- Is it authentic? Is it the student's personal goal?

- Is it realistic? Is it attainable?

- Is it significant? Does it relate in some important way to the student's life in or out of school now or in the future?

- Does the student care? Is he or she passionate about it?

Some teachers replace the heading "Importance" with "Vision." They ask students to describe the future they desire—their vision of the best they can imagine—and then show how the goal they have chosen contributes to its attainment.

The Plan

The third part of the contract is planning, which is personal curriculum development. While the process can be taught in the simplest possible way, it is also a rich field that teachers and students can explore with great benefits. The process involves selecting and sequencing the activities through which students intend to reach their goals. Here is a plan for planning:

1. Break the task into its parts.

2. Generate many ways to accomplish each part.

3. Select the ways or activities that suit your learning style, personal strengths, and interests.

4. Place these activities in the order that they must be done to complete the task.

5. Plan for organization, management, assessment, and celebration.

Sometimes the appropriate sequence is obvious. Sometimes it is dictated by the process involved when the student chooses a particular field or kind of project. Scientific investigations, constructing a building, and studying history, for example, all usually follow a required pattern, a specific process, or a preferred template. Note that the knowledge and skills required, as well as the activities to be completed, should be listed.

The Challenge

Planning may include a challenge statement or activity. It is important that the students' proposals regularly require them to reach beyond the easy and familiar to tasks that are new and demanding. Some contracts ask, "What is the challenge for you in this proposed activity?" Some require students to add a challenging step or dimension to the activity, one that pushes them to their best possible performance. Challenges that extend over a year or two are often referred to as passages. Here is a description of challenges and passages:

Challenge Activities

- Any significant first-time experience
- Any demanding activity that extends participants to new levels of performance
- The pursuit of any goal that involves a risk of failure
- Any move from the easy and familiar toward the difficult and new
- Any provocation to engage, compete, or become involved in a worthwhile activity
- Any attempt to achieve excellence

Passages

- Involve a new level of knowledge and skill and a personal change in the participant
- Mark the transition from one stage to the next, such as from adolescence to adulthood
- Extend over a longer time frame than other activities, usually a month to two years
- Are usually treated with recognition and celebration on completion

Problem Solving

Some proposal-contracts require students to examine their plans and anticipate the problems they will run into as they work. This means examining themselves and anticipating personal difficulties as well as trouble spots in the activities. The belief is that by acknowledging any tendency to procrastinate, fold in the face of difficulties, or become distracted easily, students will be more likely to do something to correct such behavior. When they acknowledge a need for information or skill, a particularly difficult task, or a risk to take, they will be more likely to make the preparations necessary to deal with them successfully. As a result, this list of problems is usually accompanied by a comparable list of proposed solutions.

Management

The management section requires students to organize a timetable that lists the major activities in the plan and the dates by which they will be completed and to list the resources needed: people they will contact, materials that will be needed, and possibly a place where the activities can be conducted.

Evaluation and Progress Measure

The evaluation section requires the student to describe the criteria by which the quality of the performance or product will be judged. In one approach, the student establishes his or her current level of performance as a baseline and then describes a minimum, satisfactory, and excellent improvement above that baseline. The theory is that having described an ordinary performance, they will avoid it in favor of pursuing the excellence they have defined. (Self-assessment is described in detail in Chapter Eight.)

Demonstration

The demonstration section requires students to describe how they will show that they have achieved their goal and the level of attainment that they proposed. By describing this demonstration at the beginning, students convert their goal into a concrete outcome, and work with that public display in mind.

Celebration

The celebration of attainment is intended to enhance students' desire for success by identifying a reward for their efforts and recognition of their achievement. It involves recognition, rewards, and special events.

Negotiating Contract Agreements

Negotiating the final form of contracts with students is a delicate interaction and a special act of teaching. The task is to ensure that contracts are worthwhile and workable without taking control away from the student. Taking a critical perspective, in which the teacher grades the contract and returns it for correction, will almost certainly be counterproductive. Think of the conference rather as a productive conversation between equals. The

---

Steps in the Contract Process

1. Think of an appropriate idea, and discuss it with your teacher.

2. When the idea is approved, write up a proposal or contract.

3. Review the contract with your advisory or support group (or both).

4. Negotiate the contract with the teacher, and if appropriate, a parent, guardian, or other parent substitute.

5. Implement the proposal. If the proposal is turning out to be too easy, too difficult, or boring, renegotiate the activity with your teacher.

6. Meet with your teacher regularly to discuss your progress.

7. Demonstrate contract completion, and celebrate your success.

8. Evaluate the project, and file proofs and assessments in the portfolio.

9. Consider your next SDL activity.

student has proposed a course of action; the conference is a time to discuss the elements, celebrate its strengths, and discuss improvements that will make it more successful and satisfying to both parties.

In formal business negotiations, the "getting to yes" process begins with both parties realizing that the outcome will not be exactly what they want but a third position to be discovered. This perspective of searching for the best approach to what the student wants to do is an excellent framework for the productive conversation. The best outcome is a contract that both teacher and student regard as promising and both look forward to enthusiastically.

These negotiations require new skills. One of the most important is learning to listen more often than you speak and to ask more often than you tell. Teachers are used to telling and directing, but in conferencing, the key skills are listening and asking. In the beginning, the main task is to help students to clarify the goals they intend to pursue and the plans they intend to follow. This means asking many questions and giving few pointed answers. The idea is to help them think and decide, not to think or decide for them. Conduct a respectful conversation with the student. Ask, and then listen to the answer. Frame the next question to push a part of that answer toward greater clarity. When a pattern emerges, summarize and ask the student for confirmation. Here is a compressed example:

Teacher: Marlene, you say you're interested in science, but what aspect of it?

Student: I'm interested in computers. I use mine a lot.

Teacher: I know you play computer games and talk with Jess and the others on e-mail, but that's not what you mean, is it?

Student: No. We're on the SETI program—the search for extraterrestrial intelligence. You know, NASA takes over our computer in downtime to help scan for messages from outer space.

Teacher: That's a passive use isn't it? What do you have in mind?

Student: I was thinking of doing something like that myself.

The Productive Teacher-Student Conversation

Teachers are most helpful to students in SDL when they help them to decide for themselves rather than decide for them. Helping students to help themselves is accomplished best in a mutually respectful conversation that moves constructively toward the clarification of ideas, the solutions to problems, or the acceptance of their proposals. Imagine stepping out of your teaching-as-telling persona and into your teaching-as-helping persona in which your task is to help students to do what they want to do and to do it well. The key is to ask great questions and confirm great replies. Set students on the course to enterprise; when they stumble, help them to find their feet and their way again. Become their partners in achievement by keeping the conversations productive. Because the risk is theirs, make it also respectful.

Teacher: You mean searching for messages from outer space?

Student: Could I gather data myself? See what it looks like? See if I can find anything?

Teacher: I'm sure it's possible. Can you think of a way?

Student: Well, I'm helping SETI. I wonder if SETI will help me.

Teacher: Can you make them an offer they can't refuse?

Student: How about getting a bunch of the others with computers together and offering them a network?

Teacher: Great idea. What will you ask them for?

Student: Some of their printout for us to look over?

Teacher: Can you think of a more active beginning?

Student: Do you think they would hook us in to receive? Could we scan for ourselves somehow?

Teacher: Why not find out? It's worth a try.

Make a question funnel like this one: go deeper and deeper, tightening the focus as you go.

Do not be afraid to confront students respectfully about what they have said if it will lead to greater clarity and focus. If you are listening closely, you will hear the inconsistencies, which will help you to guide the student back to a rational path—for example: "You said that you hate science. How are you going to do research without following a scientific approach?"

Regularly check with the student that the conference process is working. Ask, "How does this feel to you? Are we getting closer to the goals that you want to pursue? What could we do that would be more helpful?" If the process is not working, work with the student to change it.

Active listening is the key to good questions. The clues to your second question can be found only in the student's answer to your first question. Listen and respond. You will often help greatly by waiting patiently, listening closely, and expressing support for the student's plans. People understand process, develop ideas, and form commitments slowly.

A second skill that is important in negotiations is problem solving. Use it when students confront problems, and teach them to use the problem-solving approach themselves. It is tempting to use a short-cut and solve the problem for them, but rescue is disempowering. Empower them with the process. Here is a simple form of it:

1. Identify the problem as precisely as possible.

2. List all the things that might be done to solve it.

A Compressed Sample of a Student-Teacher Conference

Teacher: Hi, Alison. Have you decided what to do in your next project?

Student: Good morning, Mr. Jonas. Yes, I want to learn about the world's people.

Teacher: Very interesting. What is it about the world's people that interests you?

Student: I'm not sure. It's sort of like who they are and where they are.

Teacher: Are you thinking of a kind of survey of the different races?

Student: Yes. I want to do a map that shows where all the different kinds of people are, and then add a little description of each of them.

Teacher: What would be the challenge for you in this activity?

Student: Well, going and getting this done and then coming and talking to you about the races next week. I don't know much about it now.

Teacher: That's a good start, but that doesn't really test your abilities, does it?

Student: No, not really. I knew you'd say that. There are people from all over in this school. How about if I talk to people from different places and find out about different countries from them?

Teacher: To illustrate your research?

Student: Yes, and a map of where the countries are and where they are from.

Teacher: That sounds promising, Allison. Write that up.

---

3. Select a course of action.

4. Lay the solution out as a plan, and rehearse it mentally.

5. Solve the problem.

Encourage students to develop the habit of examining their difficulties in order to identify the specific problem that is causing them. Listing them in their journals and applying the process to them is good practice. Keep track of students with serious difficulties, and regularly check on their progress toward solutions. They may need support and assistance. Contracts can always be renegotiated.

The example that follows describes the basic elements of a negotiated contract instead of covering the full format. The other parts, such as management and assessment details, are described in other chapters.

A Negotiated Contract for a Tenth Grader's Social Studies Proposal

Subject: Social Studies. Initial Proposal.

Topic: Riots at the G-8 and other meetings of world leaders to plan global cooperation in business and finance.

Purpose: My parents are in business and talk about the riots. They think that the rioters are troublemakers who should be jailed. I think that some of them are speaking for poor people around the world who are not represented at these meetings. When I express my opinion, my parents disagree and give all kinds of reasons I am wrong that I can't argue against. I would like to know more so I can hold my own.

Proposal: To find out what these meetings and riots are all about.

The first conference between the teacher and the student, Monique, began with a discussion about the purpose of the meetings of world leaders and the causes of the riots. Then the teacher shifted the focus to Monique's proposal and exactly what she wanted to accomplish, which was to establish her own position about the riots. When the teacher asked, "What is the best outcome you can imagine?" Monique answered, "I think the rioters have a point, and if they do, maybe I can do something too." The teacher confirmed that planning some action would be a real challenge. Here are some parts of the contract that Monique submitted:

Vision: I hear a lot about globalization and a lot about what happens to poor countries and poor people who are exploited by the rich to achieve their financial gains. I think that exploitation is wrong. I want to prove that I am right. I want to know what I'm talking about and to see what can be done. I see myself doing something about it like getting some other students together to speak out.

Goal: To learn about globalization and the arguments against it that cause people to riot so that I can take a position and act on it.

Plan: Start a clipping file on articles about the G-8 and reports on the Net. Learn who the members are, what they are doing, and the effects they are having on other countries and people. Find out who the groups are that are rioting against what the G-8 are doing. Find their Web sites, make a list of who they are and their arguments. See if I can find out who causes the violence and damage and why. Figure out my position on all this, then write a position paper that I can use to express my opinions and share it with others.

Challenge: To inform others about what is going on and get a group together to discuss what we can do about it. We can at least tell someone important what we think. I may find a movement I want to join.

In the next example, we follow Geoff David, a challenging student, through his experience with the contract process. Geoff attended class sporadically and seldom handed in assignments. He was bright but passively resistant to all efforts to get him to take his studies seriously.

Mr. Dalguish presented his English course in packages leading to an accompanying major project for which each student wrote and negotiated an individual contract. During the first term, he invited his classes to attend an evening performance of a play, followed by a discussion with the director and actors. Geoff surprised him by attending and turning in his first writing assignment based on the performance. It was in the form of a song.

Mr. Dalguish saw his opportunity and took it. When he asked Geoff if he saw music in his future, Geoff replied that entertaining was his dream, but he did not think he would ever be good enough. Mr. Dalguish replied, "Geoff, you're only fifteen! Why not make composing songs your major project and see how far you can get this year? Then we'll talk about careers in music again." Geoff agreed, took the major project assignment booklet, and arranged to submit a contract the next week.

A Negotiated Contract for an Eleventh Grader's Major Project

Here is the introductory contract or proposal that Geoff submitted:

English 11: Major Project Proposal

Student: Geoff David   Parent: Constance David

Teacher: Ralph Dalguish

Outcome: To write some songs.

Reasons: I like folk and rock music. I enjoy writing songs. I hope to
   be an entertainer.

Plan: I will spend time writing songs every week.

Mr. Dalguish considered the contract far too slight and generalized to be a guide to Geoff's project for the year. To be useful, the contract had to be more detailed, more specific, and more rigorous. When they met, Mr. Dalguish asked Geoff what a songwriter could do to become skilled, and together they made a list of activities, such as finding good songs and studying them, talking to songwriters, going to workshops, as well as writing more songs and improving them. Geoff took home his assignment to write a more detailed contract and produced this second version, presented here in abbreviated form.

English 11: Major Project Contract

Student: Geoff David   Parent: Constance David

Teacher: Ralph Dalguish

Outcome: To write a collection of ten songs and present them live
   or on a tape recording.

Reasons: I enjoy writing songs and playing them. I want to become
   good at writing and playing. If I become good enough, I want to
   be an entertainer someday.

Plan: My plan has three parts.

Songwriting:

- Write a new song every two weeks (about).
- Read at least one book on writing.
- Find a songwriter to talk to (maybe on the Net?).

Guitar:

- Take three lessons (all I can afford).
- Practice at least two hours three times a week.
- Record my songs (me playing).

Recording:

- I want to (try to) use my mom's computer for editing the songs. Mr. Hock, our neighbor, says he will show me how. Don't know about this yet.
- Make a music video. A tape or CD of the songs.

Mr. Dalguish approved Geoff's contract, and Geoff began with enthusiasm, but after two weeks he became discouraged that he was unable to keep to the plan he had devised and do his regular coursework. When Mr. Dalguish realized that others in the class were having similar difficulties, he organized his students into support groups. Geoff met with a group of two other students and his teacher to discuss their plans and how they could help each other. They discussed the possibility of renegotiating their contracts to make them less demanding.

In the weeks that followed, Geoff improved his productivity, and with his project success came success in other work as well. During the presentations at the end of the year, Geoff sang three of his songs to a very favorable reception. Mr. Dalguish was impressed. "Much more than literate, Geoff. These are great songs," he wrote on his project report.

Sample Contracts

Students need practice at contract writing in order to master the process, gain confidence in themselves, and reassure themselves that they can follow their own interests with approval and support from the teacher. The teacher should keep in mind, especially in the early stages, that students will be testing the process and the teacher's real desire for them to take charge. Remember that where they begin is far from where they will arrive. Do not expect or require magnificent challenges in the beginning. Be accepting and encouraging, build a pattern of successes, and gradually raise the standard of task complexity and difficulty.

The differences in the format of the following contracts reflect the preferences of teachers and the structure of the programs or courses for which the contracts are written. The following contract, for example, was to complete one of the twelve science competencies this student, a twelfth grader, was assigned.

Conduct a scientific investigation.

Student: Paul Wang   Teacher: Brooker Campden

Subject: Science Requirement

Outcome: I want to find out why arbutus trees grow in some
     ravines but not others.

Plan: My plan is to follow the investigation process.

- Read about trees and especially the Pacific madrone (Arbutus).
  Find out how botanists do field studies.
- Inspect three sites with madrone and three without. Check
  moisture level, analyze soil, plot exposure to light, and look for
  other things.
- Use my observations to make a hypothesis about why they grow
  where they do.
- Inspect three other sites to see if the conditions are the ones I
  predicted.
- Draw conclusions about why madrone grow where they grow.
- Write up my results and present to Dr. Pettigrew. He's a botanist
  from State University.

Reasons That This Is an Important Activity: No big reason. I do a lot
     of hiking, so I'll look forward to my fieldwork. I'm just interested
     in the plants and animals and landforms around me when I'm
     out there. Botany seems like an interesting field.

This contract outline describes a fully developed contract for a major project at the senior level. Note that it is an outline of the SDL process for the development of a unit of personal curriculum. As such, it provides a schema for the teacher to follow in teaching the skills involved and a guide for the student in employing them. For the best results, begin with a simple proposal, including only a goal or outcome and a plan, and build on it systematically with teaching and practice. The contract outlines a process for SDL that students can employ for the rest of their lives to mount the learning and achievements they seek.

Here are the main parts of two other contracts:

Learning Contract for a Tenth Grader in General Science

Student: Amelia Hughes

Subject: General Science

Teacher: Toby Rigatagliano

Outcome: I want to learn how to look after sick wild animals.

Importance: We went to the zoo near my house on a field trip. I like animals and keep them. My dad nursed a hawk back to health, and we let it go out in Valecroft. I liked it a lot.

Plan: I'm going to concentrate on small mammals.

- I will read three books: one on the natural history and species of North American small mammals, one on animal physiology, and one on animal care. I will search the Internet.
- I will keep gerbils and guinea pigs and keep them alive and well.
- I will try to get work with the zoo or volunteer if I have to, cleaning up or something like that.
- I will interview our veterinarian.
- My outcome will be a guide to treating illnesses in small local wild animals.

Challenge: To work my way into the zoo so I can see how they work with animals and treat sick ones.

Amelia faced several problems as she worked on her project. Chief among them was a lack of medicine, equipment, or facilities for treating small animals. A population explosion among the gerbils was even more difficult.

Learning Contract for a Student Studying Dyslexia

Student: Jeff Ingram

Subject: To find a way to help people with dyslexia

Teacher: Gloria Abrams

Goal: To find a way to help people with dyslexia.

Importance: My sister has dyslexia but nobody diagnosed it until she was in sixth grade. She has a very hard time getting school work done. If my parents had known, we could have done something or found her help.

Plan:

- To research dyslexia.
- To observe and consult my sister.
- To confer with experts in this district and on the Internet.

Challenge: I want to develop a test for kindergartners that will diagnose them for dyslexia so they can be helped.

Jeff learned a great deal about dyslexia and especially about the importance of early intervention. He worked with a kindergarten class trying out different approaches to diagnosis and finally found that a check of their ability to follow instructions showed early signs of the dysfunction. His test was to convince teachers that the test he devised could help them to identify and to accommodate the problem. He did, and two teachers attended his presentation to the school board to testify.

Tracking Student Progress

It is important for students to know that they have responsibilities and that someone is keeping track of what they are doing and how well they are doing it. It is equally important for teachers to know what every student is doing and how well each is progressing so that they can be sure that everyone is moving forward. The key issue is allocation of time. With everyone pursuing different activities, it is important to know what students intend to do and what they are actually doing. Records of these details will show which students are active and which are not and which students are progressing and which need assistance.

Keeping track has three phases: students record what they intend to do, teachers take note of what they are actually doing, and then teachers decide who most needs assistance to move forward or to get back on track.

The first step is setting up a procedure for students to record what they intend to do in the form of an agreement or contract for a particular period of work. This period varies depending on the activity and the situation. It may be a month or even a year if a student is working on a graduation passage or challenge. Geoff David, in the example above, worked for more than a year on his challenge to become skillful enough to play his music for others. He recorded his work schedule in his contract. When he could not keep to it and realized that even the work he scheduled was inadequate for progressing as he planned, it was time for the teacher to intervene and call a conference with Geoff to restructure his program. In his case, the conference involved his parents too. The teacher must be alert for such ripe moments. Many students are too ambitious or not ambitious enough, and they need to refocus and reschedule their work in the light of what they have learned about themselves and their chosen tasks.

Common units of planning are a day or a week. At Thomas Haney, each student records a plan for that day. When an individual teacher is involved rather than a whole school, a computer file can be set up for each day with the date and a list of the students' names. Students type in brief summaries of their work plans. Two or more computers can be networked to speed up the process. If computers are not available, a planning sheet with the date and names can be circulated and later entered in a class book. A third alternative is to use individual planning books. Students keep these booklets open or available so that teachers can see what was planned and what is actually being done at the same time as they circulate. Exhibit 6.2 shows two examples of student entries for a day's work at Thomas Haney, first for a week and then for the day.

EXHIBIT 6.2

A Tenth Grader's Plans for a Week and for a Day

WEEKLY PLAN

Priorities and Goals for the Week of September 30–October 6

	Subject	Learning Guide Number	Priority/Goal
1	Science	2	Complete questions and chart of star life cycle
2	French	1	Prepare for test and take it
3	Math	1	CD program. Text chap. 2 and problems
4	Social Studies	2	See video, take notes, decide argument
5	English	2	Read *All Quiet;* see movie
6	Gym		Tennis backhand
7	Band		Practice

DAILY PLAN

Tuesday, October 6   **Day Plan**   **Teaching Assistant Approval: RG**

Time	Subject	Learning Guide Number	Activities	Work Place	Adviser's Initials
8:48	Science	2	Life cycle of stars. Video. Notes	Lab	
9:55	Social Studies	2	Copy notes. Hand in	100 G	
10:52	Band	-	Practice	B Rm	
1:35	French		Study for test	100 G	
2:41	Math		Activity 4. Get CD.	Lib.	

Meetings and Clubs:	Sign up for foods lab
Important Reminders:	Basketball game, away
Homework:	Read *All Quiet on W. Frnt*

Source: *Reproduced with permission from Thomas Haney High School, Maple Ridge, British Columbia, Canada.*

EXHIBIT 6.3

Samples from a Teacher's Observation Sheet

Names	Observation 1	Observation 2
Abrams, Charles	Doing hands-on math	Same
Bronski, Marci	Working with support team (physics robot project)	Writing report (vocation)
Chan, Eleanor	Daydreaming	Socializing

The second part of keeping track is noting what students are actually doing. The simplest way is to make up an observation sheet on which the students' names are listed, along with a small space for quick notes summarizing two or three observations and brief conferences. Attach the sheet to a clipboard, and circulate through the classroom. See what everyone is doing, perhaps in a quick survey; make brief notes; and then return to those who need special attention. If everyone is progressing, hold conferences or meet with students who can benefit from assistance. Exhibit 6.3 shows the beginning of a sample observation sheet.

It's not hard to see who needs help and fast. The teacher needs to find out what is happening. Be neutral until you know. A child who appears to be daydreaming may have been up all night writing a play. Here are a few other ways of keeping track that are used in different schools and classrooms:

- Meet regularly with advisory groups of students to check and discuss progress.

- Place the responsibility on students to check in regularly to report their progress and ensure that they are on track.

- Call seminar meetings with groups of students who are experiencing similar difficulties or to introduce new opportunities or skills.

Once students have employed contracts and mastered the process, teachers may wish to use a simpler form of reporting. Students will develop their focus, plans, and arrangements as entries in their working journals (see Chapter Seven for details about the working journal). The final act is to secure the student's commitment to the work she or he has contracted to complete. Once that is done, students get to work, and the teacher's role shifts again to supervisor, guide, and counselor. The script is written, the curtain goes up, but the play is just beginning. The question is, "What keeps the actors moving and why?" The answer is motivation.

Chapter 7

Motivating and Empowering Students

MOTIVATION is both a unique and critical issue in teaching adolescents to be self-directed. It is unique in that the teacher must motivate students to take on the task of managing their own activities and must then teach them to motivate themselves as an essential aspect of continuing self-direction. It is unique in that we are dealing with adolescence, a dynamic and sometimes troubled stage in students' lives. Our efforts are most successful when they help students to manage the tasks their development is presenting to them. Students often begin SDL activities with enthusiasm and then hit the wall of responsibility and become disheartened, a discouraging event to both students and teachers. It is critical to anticipate this possibility and be ready to respond to it as an important teaching opportunity rather than as a sign that the program is failing or that the student is hopeless.

Some students begin with prior experience in and a proclivity for self-direction; others arrive with little experience of personal responsibility and a dependence on direction from others. Those not ready must be identified quickly and given special guidance. As with any other adolescent group, some such students will be especially difficult, and the teacher must be ready to respond appropriately. Fortunately, the dynamics of the SDL process itself provides the teacher with a framework for dealing with all of these issues successfully.

Encouraging Students to Pursue SDL

The first principle of motivation in SDL is to build enthusiasm among students for involvement in the process. At the beginning, especially if the program's students are volunteers, the teacher should present SDL as an outstanding choice, one full of opportunities, challenges, and benefits. He or she could display posters summarizing the program and its advantages to students, and collect slides of student work in previous classes for a show of what is possible. Including previous students and parents in a promotional meeting and securing their endorsement can also be influential to students and beneficial to the program. Resource G at the back of this book offers many ideas for promoting the SDL experience.

The second principle is modeling SDL. The teacher should be a model of the process—one who is committed to it and is actively employing it. One SDL teacher, for example, used his efforts to become a published writer as a model for the process with his students. They followed his progress with interest and especially the difficulties he faced and how he responded. At every turn, he not only taught them by his example, but he also learned what his students faced in their struggles to be self-directed.

A third principle of motivation for SDL is creating a positive climate that nurtures student productivity. That environment should be stimulating, nonthreatening, inviting, and positive, with an ever-changing visual provocation to think and act. Pictures, posters, charts, and examples of work should abound. Stations should be available for computing, reading, small group meetings, and any special activities of the course or field. While imposed competition is threatening, competition chosen, competition in teams, or competition with oneself is generally a positive stimulation. Students must believe that they can be successful in the enterprises they undertake. This begins with setting a warm, respectful, businesslike tone in teacher-student interactions. It means teachers communicating to students their confidence in the students' ability to be successful but always backed up by the training and guidance that makes success probable.

A fourth general principle of motivating student involvement and progress in SDL is providing initial or sustaining adventures and using them as metaphors for the challenges presented. Any first-time dramatic experience will serve this purpose. When location permits, a camping experience provides everyone with responsibilities, requires independence on the part of participants, and encourages bonding as a special group. Such an experience gives students who usually do not shine in classroom work a chance to contribute and excel. Service activities such as working with the elderly, those who are disabled, or young children can also provide a rewarding experience. Choosing a charity and conducting an urban hike, bike ride, or work project with each student sponsored for how far he or she goes or does is another approach. No matter what challenge is presented, an orientation to it and a meeting to debrief the significance of the activity later are essential.

A fifth principle of motivation for students of SDL is to adapt the course or program to the students' experience of adolescence and the demands it places on them. Adolescence is a distinctive state. We know that many teens experience growth spurts and hormonal storms, and now the latest research shows that the adolescent brain goes through a period of chaotic adjustment too. Students must take on the task of developing the person they will be, establishing new kinds of relationships with others, becoming independent and competent, shaping their values and character, and beginning the transition to more adult-like behavior.

Fortunately, the features of SDL are well matched to the demands of adolescence. They require students to learn in a way that promotes these transformations and this transition. The freedoms and responsibilities, the challenges and relationships, the lifelong skills and processes, and the accomplishments that students experience all make SDL a training ground for the successful completion of the psychosocial adolescent agenda. Make that agenda a guide to course design, construction, and interaction. Treat students with respect, acknowledge their challenging journey, encourage independence, recognize mature behavior, and celebrate all achievement.

These five principles—selling SDL, modeling it, creating a positive environment for it, introducing dramatic experiences, and matching the program to the demands of adolescence—comprise a dynamic framework for motivating students to adopt SDL and to be successful in pursuing it.

Anyone coming to an SDL classroom for the first time could surely think there is a lack of discipline here. No lineups. No bells. Kids coming and going. But that's all out here. We're concerned about what's going on inside them. Their sense of purpose and direction. Their ability to manage themselves. The thoughtfulness that they show to others. That's the discipline we care about. [Karla Myles, former principal of Jefferson County Open School]

Motivating Students to Motivate Themselves

The key to self-direction is encouraging students to design and accomplish their own learning tasks and then motivating them to motivate themselves to learn. This is possible because SDL is designed to motivate. It offers a transition from control by others to control of oneself. Freedom is given as responsibility is taken. Students learn to find and pursue their interests, to struggle and achieve, and to demonstrate their achievements and reap the rewards. They learn about themselves by finding out what they can do and become. They learn about others, find companionship, and see themselves as they are seen by the many individuals and groups they experience. And they learn about the world and how to move through it competently.

Recognition by students that the program is dealing with their issues will gradually emerge, and teachers can help that process by connecting the activities to their greater purposes. As students take control, for example, they should realize that it is an adult act and a step toward maturity. Be your students' challenge cheerleader. Above all, sell competence. Competence is its own reward. Do whatever you can to get them to taste the pleasures of skill. The advantages of life go to the competent, along with the pleasures of the experience and the admiration of others.

In *Motivating Humans* (1992), Martin Ford outlines the main principles of motivation that he derived from research. The greatest motivator is the active pursuit of personal interests in real circumstances. On these grounds, SDL is a highly motivating program. As students master the processes of SDL, they are learning how to motivate themselves by discovering their interests, finding compelling ways to pursue them, and sustaining their efforts to a rewarding conclusion. One success encourages them to pursue another.

The key to helping students become self-starters is teaching them to turn inward, to hear their own voices instead of the crowd's, and to conduct conversations with themselves about the decisions they must make. To do that, they may have to silence the insistent voices of parents, teachers, and friends that ring in their minds telling them what to think and what they should do. As emerging adults, students must discover and develop themselves, identifying their own thoughts and feelings and setting their own course into the future. Achieving clarity about oneself is essential for success in SDL and is the motivation that drives it. Teachers can stoke the fires of their students' self-motivation in such ways as the following:

• *Help students to find and pursue a passion.* The most recurrent theme among SDL teachers is the importance of helping students to find something that interests them, something that is their own, something that is full of promise. Expose them to a variety of experiences in a variety of situations.

• *Help students to translate interests into clear and compelling goals.* As Ford suggests, specific, desirable goals are essential. Without them, there is no motivation. Once a passion has been identified, the next step is to translate it into specific goals that can be acted on. Competencies and challenges provide a general framework within which each student can find personal focus and effort. By learning to set their own goals, students also learn to motivate themselves. The learning contract and major challenges or graduation passages focus students on the task. Make sure that the goals are stated so clearly that the student and anyone else reading them know what needs to be done. Be sure that each goal is the student's own and that it is compelling. If several goals are tied together in a single enterprise, motivation is even stronger.

• *Connect students with at least one person who cares about them.* Students in SDL need to know that there are people who care about them specifically, and especially one person who is directly connected with them and their progress. Belonging to a community is important, but a special contact is critical. In many programs, this person is the adviser with whom they meet regularly in an advisory group and individually at least twice a week. As an adviser, be available, connect, support, counsel, and guide. At Jefferson County Open, the program begins with each advisory group taking a camping trip together so that such special connections can begin. If you can, tie troubled students into a network of supportive people: a counselor, a peer support team, an admired senior student, a sponsor from the community, a mentor from an apprenticeship work site. Such students need to know someone who cares is watching, that they are expected to succeed, and that there is plenty of support to make sure they do.

• *Deal with each student as an individual in an individual situation.* Many students will have unique issues to deal with in order to become self-directed. Some have issues at home, others with peers, and still others in dealing with themselves that impede their progress. Monique may be running from her stepmother's abuse, Bill may be in trouble with the police, Angie may be spoiled helpless, and Sangit may be in cultural crisis. These issues must be resolved by the students themselves, but they need the opportunity to talk, confirmation that they are okay, and guidance in developing alternative strategies for resolution.

• *Provide feedback to students, and teach them to secure feedback for themselves.* The effort to achieve goals flags without specific, accurate, and helpful feedback. Students not only need feedback, they also need to know that it is coming. Conferences provide a good opportunity for feedback, but be sure that they guide improvement and are perceived as useful. SDL programs are designed to build in several feedback systems: peer support groups, meetings, advisory group sessions, teacher-student conferences, working with mentors, involvement in community activities, demonstrations, and celebrations. Teach them to ask for feedback and to determine from the results of their initiatives which ones are successful and which are not, and why. Feedback motivates by naming successes, identifying problems, and suggesting solutions. Without feedback, students lose their way and their momentum. It feels as if no one cares.

• *Challenge students appropriately, and teach them to challenge themselves.* Challenge students in activities they value. Challenge is an invitation to break out of limits, to exercise one's strengths, to know one's power. A pattern of successfully meeting challenges leads to a sense of efficacy. When we ask students to write contracts, we invite them to challenge themselves to reach new levels of performance that they can only imagine. We invite them to test and to realize their powers. But we must be careful that the challenge is neither so great that it is unattainable nor so trivial that it is not worth doing. Challenge should be difficult but possible for the individual.

Recent research has made it clear that we need challenge throughout our lives if we wish to develop our mental capacities thoroughly and to retain our alertness into old age. It is also clear that challenging ourselves to do things that we value is the major means by which people learn when schooling ends. Successfully meeting challenges also confirms our talents, reassures us that we can meet what challenges lie ahead, and lifts us to a higher platform from which we can see even greater challenges ahead.

• *Encourage students to identify their strengths and to employ them as often as possible.* All students have strengths that they can identify. Their strength may be in relationships, athletics, artistic expression, character, assertiveness, languages, humor, organization, caring, construction, reliability, or any among hundreds of others. In *Now, Discover Your Strengths* (2001), Marcus Buckingham and Donald Clifton identify thirty-four themes of strength based on a Gallup study of over 2 million people and then propose that everyone can learn best by building on their five signature strengths. Students may take Gallup's Strengthfinder.com Profile on-line or simply determine for themselves what they do well, what strengths they bring to anything they do, and what others would say were their powers. Using a group to anonymously list each other's strengths is also a good group builder. Make your own class list of SDL strengths, and keep it displayed on a chart (see the personal performance profile in Chapter Eight).

• *Ensure that every student experiences success.* Success motivates. When we see that we can complete a task, we are ready to do it again; when we do it well and are acknowledged, we want to do it again. If it is a success we want and achieve it after a struggle, we cannot wait to do it again. If the success was also exhilarating and earned us praise, we will do anything to do it again. Sequences of such successes, especially when they are occasionally interrupted with difficulties that are overcome, are life altering. They are the threads that compose the fabric of our lives and shape the images that define who we are.

Create successes by employing gradients of intensity in assigned work and encouraging students to set units of work that are attainable. Provide many pathways. Urge students to employ their strengths. Convert one overwhelming task into a sequence of easier ones, and urge them to do the same. Evaluate so that each student has an opportunity to succeed, such as by measuring progress against personal baselines or by seeking validation letters (letters by sponsors and mentors testifying to the accomplishments of students under their supervision). Celebrate achievement; be sure that everyone is celebrated.

• *Help all students to become competent in achieving their goals and, if possible, to become an expert in a field of their own choice.* Competence is the ability to generate the skillful outcomes that are deemed successful. The deeper reward is becoming absorbed, going beneath the surface of things. In *Creativity* (1996), Mihaly Csikszentmihalyi describes this feeling of contented absorption as flow, the effortless involvement in intense activity for the quality of experience it provides. We also experience such absorption when we exercise skills expertly in challenging projects.

Teach students to be skillful—and expert, if possible—in a special field of choice. Every child should be working on becoming absorbed and competent in a field of activity that gives them pleasure. The balance of curriculum coverage is depth of study. While it is important to learn something about everything, it is equally important to know everything about something or to come as close as possible to that goal.

• *Never stop trying to motivate students or to teach them to motivate themselves.* There are many ways to motivate students, and far more than we can cover here. Somewhere there is an approach, an experience, or a comment that will click, and the student will be on the move. Never give up.

It is difficult to be civil to students when they are resistant and objectionable. In such instances, however, treating students respectfully is critical, especially since we want them to respect themselves and then others. When you do not give up or become resentful, students see what is happening. They know that the door is staying open. These guidelines for motivating students are also guidelines for cultivating and maintaining the drive for continual, life-long learning.

The Working Journal as a Motivational Tool

The most important book students will ever read is their working journal, and they will be its author. A working journal is a handbook for the productive person and is modeled on the journals often kept by artists, writers, scientists, explorers, historians, politicians, inventors, businesspeople, athletes, educators, and architects for recording their ideas and activities. For SDL students too, it is the handbook in which they store their thoughts, work out their plans, and record the struggles and progress they experience in pursuit of their self-directed work. The book invites thinking and action, it is a constant confidant and guide, and it quickly becomes a record of obstacles overcome and successes achieved. As the main space where students talk to themselves, the journal is an important instrument for motivation, especially self-motivation. (For a sample of a working journal, see Resource I.)

A working journal is really several kinds of books in one. It is a notebook of useful and interesting information. It is a sketchbook and journal of original thoughts, ideas, comments, and designs, such as the one Leonardo da Vinci kept. It is a planner for the keeper's projects and a log of events in the history of his or her activities. It is a reflective diary in which the performer stands back to consider ways that the performance and the performer can be improved. Finally, it is a historical overview in which the project is considered within the framework of the student's life in general.

The working journal is also a machine for productivity. In that machine, the main parts are thinking, planning, acting, reviewing, and renewing. When these parts mesh and gather momentum, they generate productive power, a profound feeling of personal control, and great hope and pride. When students think through to a good idea, generate a plan for pursuing the idea, learn to put the plan into action successfully, and see how to develop even greater success in the future, their lives will never be the same again.

The journal is an excellent medium for teaching all the skills basic to researching, thinking, creating, planning, acting, and reflecting. It also helps supervisors to monitor student progress, understand their problems, and assess their achievement. On a cautionary note, the journal is of little use if students do not make their entries genuine expressions of the struggles they have faced and the feelings they have experienced, and many are unlikely to be genuine if they know that the whole of their journal is open to scrutiny. Students also have rights to privacy and therefore are in control of their journals. Teachers will be wise to negotiate the conditions of journal review in the beginning and to adhere to the agreement rigorously. Trust is vital in this process.

Everything in the working journal contributes to the student's enterprises in SDL. Students collect useful information and ideas. This is where interests are discovered and nourished. The information and ideas that they find in books, on the Internet, in conversations, and in class are important, but even more valuable are the student's own ideas, observations, and arguments. These explorations lead to the student's goals and plans for activities they will undertake, and once the action is under way, the journal becomes the place to record its history, including the problems that come up and the solutions that are introduced to resolve them. Finally, the journal is the place where students record their thoughts about their work, their performance, and themselves. Learning is about change, development, and productivity. Through reflection, students become truly self-directional. They see themselves more clearly, understand better what their personal authentic choices are, and see their choices within the perspective of their lives. It is the individual's handbook of SDL.

Dealing with the SDL Crisis

Becoming self-directed is not easy. There is much for students to learn about managing their tasks and about managing themselves. Some students who have experience in self-direction or a proclivity for it will readily adapt to the process. Others who are dependent, have low self-esteem, or come fresh from a pattern of failure in other classes will find it difficult and need special assistance. Many students begin with enthusiasm, but when the responsibilities accumulate, some falter. When that happens, some students accept their failure as their own and become discouraged. Others may blame the program or the teacher for their difficulties, and complain. If this condition continues without treatment, a crisis can develop for students, the teacher, and the program.

This crisis is a predictable event, and so it is important to take steps to prevent it and be ready with solutions that will help students through it successfully. The prevention is to introduce the skills and responsibilities of SDL gradually. The solution, when the crisis occurs, is to regard it not as a failure of the program but as an important teaching moment. The crisis brings the difficulties involved into sharp focus. This enables the teacher to identify them, focus on them, and guide the student through them. When students make it through successfully, they will later regard the event as one of the most important experiences of the course, if not of their learning lives.

If students are simply turned loose to achieve course outcomes or course projects on their own, the course is in jeopardy. When we instead gradually introduce students to the tasks and the skills they need to achieve them, we give them the opportunity to be successful. In such a graduated approach, we begin with a high degree of teacher direction in completing course outcomes; as students become skillful, we gradually withdraw direction until they can achieve them on their own and the transition is complete. Gradualism is the key. Pursue the outcomes together as a class, then in small groups, and finally as individuals. Make initial tasks simple and easy, and gradually increase the level of difficulty and complexity. In self-direction, especially in self-directed activities that are challenging, problems always arise. Giving up is one of the most common traps. Teach students to be proud of their ability to identify and resolve the difficulties they confront.

By preparing them thoroughly and introducing tasks and skills gradually, teachers minimize the crises students will face and lay the groundwork for getting them through the crises that cannot be avoided.

The crises that students experience seem to follow a pattern. It is not universal, but it is common enough to merit our examination. Although a particular experience of it may vary, many of the stages in the pattern will appear in some form with many students, and the responses we describe will prove useful. Anticipating the crises enables teachers to avoid them or to help students through them, and it also enables teachers to remain calm, confident, and positive when that is difficult but necessary. In SDL as in the rest of life, problems abound, and these kinds of issues will arise. The responses that we suggest in dealing with the various stages should be helpful in motivating students to address their difficulties and in guiding them through to success.

Decision

Students who are in an SDL class because they chose to be often begin with high expectations. When students enter a class unaware that SDL is involved, teachers often begin with an introduction that also raises expectations. Students usually begin in anticipation but in ignorance of the rigors ahead. The teacher can help to prepare students in a number of ways. One is to tell the story of a famous self-directed person, such as civil rights activist Martin Luther King, Jr., Israeli prime minister Golda Meier, or golf champion Tiger Woods. One excellent example is the Wright brothers, Wilbur and Orville. With only a high school education and no sign of exceptional talent, these two bicycle shop owners systematically solved the problems of powered flight, previously abandoned by highly trained engineers as impossible, and at Kittyhawk in 1903 they flew their famous biplane for the first time. It was an exceptional self-directed learning project.

Such stories provide a vivid introduction to the process. Discussions might conclude with Winston Churchill's six-word graduation speech to an eastern American college: "Never give up! Never give up!"

Initial Excitement

New experiences are exciting, especially when they offer new freedoms and many opportunities for interesting, adventuresome learning. Students often begin the program eagerly. They enjoy having their own space, being free to move around and talk, and setting up interesting activities. Some take on huge projects through misjudgment or in an attempt to impress both peers and adults and then plunge into the task. Others set minimum goals and defend their value heatedly. They dabble and socialize. These excesses represent both poles of the spectrum of misconception of an SDL project.

At this point, the challenge is to maintain the excitement but also to nudge the student who is responding excessively into a more appropriate level of intensity. The individual conference or meetings with the support group and advisory group offer excellent opportunities. While discussing the learning contract, for example, the teacher can raise the issue of task intensity and discuss the task and its magnitude.

Recognition

As students pursue their SDL projects, they soon experience the magnitude of the task; many are shocked at the enormity of it. Gradually, they realize all that they have to learn and accomplish, the difficulties that they have to overcome, the arrangements they have to make, the people they have to work with, and the visibility of their success or failure in accomplishing what they set out to do. This shock is a reasonable response for any dependent, disorganized, or casual student and may occur to students of any capability. It breeds in them feelings of confusion and doubt, but it is a normal stage—and an important one—in the progress toward accomplishment in SDL. This trauma of freedom is the recognition of the responsibilities that go with increased autonomy, the same responsibilities they must learn to assume as they approach adulthood.

The key responses here are clarification without accusation and assistance without rescue. The challenge is to identify problems and consider solutions. Clarify the new teacher and student roles they are experiencing. Help the student to analyze exactly what is happening; conduct a detailed review, asking them to identify what is working and what is not.

Follow a pattern that they can use themselves for troubleshooting in the future. Start with the students' intentions and goals. Are they too ambitious or too trivial? Have they pursued a real interest or what they think they are expected to pursue? Follow the steps in the process. When the problems are identified, list them. When the review is complete, choose a key obstacle, and encourage the student to generate solutions. Choose the best solution, and expand it into a plan.

During this process, the teacher may observe that the student needs certain important attitudes, concepts, or skills. (An excellent time to teach them is when they are most needed.) One skill that often seems lacking but necessary for students is self-management: setting personal goals, drawing up a prioritized list of tasks, creating a timetable, and monitoring progress. These approaches can also be taught to support groups so students can help each other to avoid difficulties or work through them. Let students know that their struggle is real and normal and that by understanding and resolving the challenge of responsibility now, they are preparing for a successful adulthood.

Crisis

In this stage, surprise turns to abandonment in hopelessness or resistance and avoidance in anger. Some will be immobilized by the complexity of their self-directed tasks, fail to meet deadlines, or perform at a level much below the one they anticipated. The crisis intensifies until they must deal with their failure. Some will blame themselves, feel hopeless, and become lethargic; others will become hostile and blame the teacher or the program. Whether students internalize or externalize their reactions, a calm, confident response is essential. Students must be guided through this crisis.

When responding to students in difficulty, take nothing personally. Keep the focus on this critical issue and on helping students to resolve it in a way that prepares them to deal more successfully with the next problem or crisis when it arrives. Ask for and listen empathetically to the students' concerns. Acknowledge them and move to solutions. This may be a good time to renegotiate the learning contract to make it more manageable or to consider a new activity. Help students to recall a time when they faced such difficulties and worked through them successfully. Using this experience as a model, explore what attitudes and strategies accounted for their success, and then transfer them to the current situation. Revisit this hope, vision, or dream for the activity under way. Then take a piece of the old goal and plan to complete it as a separate activity. Breaking the plan into sections around subgoals as separate challenges enables students to address each one more hopefully. Arrange for students to work with an admired peer or small group in the class. Consider setting a brief high-interest activity to give them a success from which to move forward.

Students who internalize their difficulty and blame themselves may benefit from a counseling approach in which the teacher encourages them to discuss the feelings they are experiencing. Listen and respond without judgment. Help them to identify the feelings and the aspects of the situation from which they arose. Help them to test the truth of assumptions they may have about their inability to handle such situations: set another task together, and help the student to complete it successfully. The transition to successful self-direction means replacing "No, I can't" assumptions with "Yes, I can" affirmations. Changing negative assumptions begins with hard evidence of positive results.

Realism

In this stage, students accept the reality of the difficulties involved in SDL. They recognize what is required from them to overcome these obstacles and acknowledge the advantages of becoming skilled at solving their own problems. In the best scenario, students convert the experience of overcoming their difficulties into valuable lessons. They develop a clearer picture of what they can accomplish and accept the need to get organized right away and work steadily even though no one is pushing them to get at it. This state of readiness is the turning point in the transition to productivity.

This is an important opportunity for the teacher to confirm and nurture this transition. Encourage students to write about their difficulties and success in their journals and to share their struggles and resolutions with others in groups or with the class. Celebrate them. Underscore these achievements with personal comments and in comments on the student's contracts—comments that can be included in their portfolios and can be seen at home. Reaffirm the value of challenge, struggle, achievement, and personal growth.

Commitment and Achievement

After their struggles, students become successful in their SDL activities and more committed to its practices and principles. As they become more self-disciplined, systematic, and effective and begin to achieve the outcomes they seek, they will also begin to report positive changes in themselves, and their parents will begin to report such changes at home. They will report feelings of empowerment, satisfaction, and pride.

This is the time to confirm, celebrate, and move forward. One excellent way to confirm and celebrate is to conduct the first self-evaluation conference with students and their parents. Organize for one to four students to be reporting on their progress at one time, each telling about their difficulties and their final achievements. This group session will also allay the fears that parents of struggling students may have about the program. Then move students on to the next task with new contracts and more challenging endeavors. Problems will still arise but will seldom be so devastating again.

Plateau and Remobilization

After a period of success, students may tend to relax, feel comfortable, and slack off. They resist new challenges and rest on their laurels from past achievements and pause. This pause is often deserved, but it is not uncommon for students to settle in so deeply that they need to be pried out of the nest again.

Keeping track of student activities daily on an observation sheet provides an indicator of where individuals are in their progress and where the class is generally. It provides an early warning system for detecting problems and slowdowns. When students slack off, distinguish catching their breath between efforts from slowing down in effort altogether. When a slowdown occurs, the time is at hand to remobilize either the individual students concerned or the class in general. This may be a time for firm insistence on performance, for challenging contracts and dramatic action. Confront students who are proposing familiar, comfortable, and easy projects. Introduce a provocative stimulus. Invite former students to return and talk to the class. Introduce a class project such as a science trip to a new environment for field studies or conservation activities. Organize an adventure or a retreat to reenergize the class.

Working with Difficult Students

In SDL programs, students usually have the freedom to think independently, learn in their own way, and move when and where they choose within the classroom and often beyond it. Such freedoms can exist only if students exercise them responsibly. The responsible exercise of freedom requires maturity and inner control, characteristics that many high school students have not yet developed. The conditions necessary for SDL enable students to be difficult and enable difficult students to be more difficult. The issues of inner control, responsibility, and maturity are placed on the table from the first day, along with the opportunity to learn and practice them. They comprise a major theme, benefit, and outcome of SDL. For teachers, addressing the issue of self-control is important, practicing patience while students learn to be responsible is necessary, and acknowledging and rewarding mature behavior when it occurs is essential. Extend freedom as students earn it. Even more important, cultivate self-motivation. Cultivate their desire to be self-directed in order to achieve a desirable future. Self-motivation is the bridge to self-management especially for difficult students.

Try to create a cooperative atmosphere by establishing with the class basic operating guidelines, procedures, and manners. Reach agreements, make them public, and live by them. Balance freedoms with responsibilities, and make exercising freedoms dependent on meeting responsibilities. For seriously delinquent behavior, the consequence can be the loss of classroom freedoms and finally the loss of the SDL program itself. Fortunately, the SDL process is an excellent antidote to delinquent behavior. Help students find a passion, get them to success, and then build on their new strengths. Get them on the path to self-esteem. When students become actively involved in interesting fields and gain recognition for it, they soon become too busy to be difficult.

Following are five ways to work with difficult students that teachers can build into their SDL programs. Everyone's approach is different, of course, so the task is to build one that suits your manner and style.

1. *Make the behavior that is expected from students very clear.* Whether you state what is required or it is determined cooperatively in a class discussion, make a clear statement of the expected behavior. List the guidelines agreed on, outline procedures for taking action, and describe the manners expected in their interactions with each other. Then teach them. Go over the list, discuss the items, clarify the meaning, and rehearse the behavior involved. Keep everything as simple and reasonable as possible. Anticipate problems and develop solutions: require plans for the period's or day's work, have a sign-up list and time limits for scarce equipment, and develop a permission slip for out-of-class or out-of-school activities. Allow an orientation period. Organize cooperation; do not enforce obedience.

2. *Target individual, difficult students for specific transformative experiences.* Here are some examples of how teachers reached individual students:

- Billy's teacher tried everything imaginable to get him involved, but he willfully resisted everything and continued his disruptive ways until one day she sent him to work with a class in the primary grades. The children loved him, he went back many times, did a passage working with troubled children, and became a different person.

- When Mrs. Grail suggested that "Mad Dog" Martine and his border collie attend obedience school, her plan worked: Mad Dog learned discipline too and was proud of it.

- Ms. Barr invited two of her promising but troubled students to her home for an elegant dinner with candles, classical music, and a tough reading assignment "to ensure a stimulating dinner conversation." She gave them a marvelous crash course in a cultural lifestyle they knew nothing about. "Instead of punishing them, I fed them. The poor boys never recovered. They did the most amazing things," she said.

- Mr. Melvin took Amber, his most difficult student, to a Rotary meeting and asked her to speak in his place about the SDL program she was in. He said that it was a risk, but he knew it was all right when Amber began, "Any program that can put up with me being in it has to have a lot going for it."

Teachers can also use their own subjects as a resource for transformative experiences:

- Marcia Stankowski insists that her English and drama students see a compelling play performance in the theater or act in one for an audience.

- Mark Hatcher takes his earth science students on field trips to study landforms and collect mineral specimens. "Different kids get hooked in the field," he says. "I give the difficult kids responsibilities and bargain with them that if all goes well this time, we'll do more trips later."

3. *Help every student to find the special experience that makes everything seem possible.* Give students a sense of importance, and offer them a place to shine. If students cannot find the experience they need, find it for them.

Tough kids respond to heroes—especially sports heroes. I encouraged one group to write fan letters to players on local teams. The kids labored over these letters and were thrilled when players responded, and most did. One even accepted an invitation to join the kids for a street hockey game. We kept a record of players' performances, worked out their stats, and started a corner for responses and memorabilia. It's a winner. [Brian Hodgins, retired special education teacher]

4. *Become a counselor, and help students to overcome the difficulties that are making them classroom problems.* Consider the problem behavior a learning opportunity: make dealing with it an SDL activity. Meet with students individually. Student-teacher conferences over learning proposals offer excellent opportunities to explore and discuss any difficulties that students are experiencing. Many students, for example, may have difficulty making decisions about their work and the commitment necessary to see the work through. One of the strengths of SDL is that it raises learning issues that are life issues too. Help students to identify and examine the issues that disturb them, consider alternatives, and then adopt new approaches. The very dependent student who has learned to succeed by doing exactly what teachers want may be a problem when what the teacher wants is an authentic personal decision. Aggressive students may be frustrated by the reflective thought required in SDL to reach any kind of decision. Remember that the quietly helpless are as difficult as those who act out loudly. Reshape the activities to help them. Make the early activities brief; decide with students before they decide on their own. Find a way; there always is one.

If what you're doing isn't working, stop doing it, and try something else. Reframe: rethink the situation. Ask, "When were things better than this? What would be happening if things were better now?" Remember when you were successful with this kind of kid before, and draw on that experience. If you haven't been successful before, find someone to advise you who has. [Gary Phillips, educational consultant]

5. *Involve the difficult student in a network of social interaction.* Students who participate in trips at Jefferson County Open give firm testimony to the power of sustained social interaction with peers and teachers to have a powerful influence on student behavior. As one student observed, "You can fake it at school, but you can't fake it working together ten hours a day for two weeks cleaning up a farm wrecked by a flood. Working, eating, sleeping together, we talk, and sooner or later you have to face who you are and what you are doing." Any positive social connection helps. The support group can be a crucible for personal change, and the advisory group can help. Working in teams provides opportunities for social practice and feedback. Experiences with adults at school and in the community can also provide students with guiding models and experiences. Create a social network that will guide students into healthy, productive patterns.

These approaches assume that although they may be difficult to work with, students can be reached through a teacher's thoughtful efforts. This is not always the case. Occasionally a student will be out of control because of medical or emotional problems that are beyond the scope of the practices discussed here. In such cases, the teacher should draw upon all of the resources available in the school and the community to find the most appropriate response. Counselors, doctors, or psychiatrists can help students gain self-control with pharmaceutical prescriptions, therapy, or other methods not available to the teacher. Provide the support and encouragement students need while they are adjusting to these methods.

•   •   •

Motivation is the engine that drives learning. Do everything possible to engage students in SDL. Help them find the determination to work through their first confrontations with the difficulties involved in directing themselves. As they begin to achieve successes, confirm their accomplishments, and use their success to teach them to employ the SDL process to motivate themselves. Conduct that process as a motivational activity, and be ready to focus on troubled students with a repertoire of responses that will help them to find a pathway to achievements that will give them the pride and self-esteem they need to change.

Chapter 8

Assessing Student Achievement

THE APPROPRIATE ASSESSMENT for SDL is student self-assessment. In self-assessment, students evaluate the complete process of action learning from conception through performance to the outcome or product. Students assess themselves because it is an essential skill for successful self-direction. It is meta-learning; learning how to learn includes learning how to assess how well one is learning. It provides the questions that students must always have in mind: "Is this the right task for me to be doing now?" "Am I doing it well?" and "Is this a worthy result?" Self-assessment applies not only to individual activities or courses, but also to the overall educational and life programs that students are shaping for themselves. It is essential that the SDL student regularly ask, "Is what I am doing a demonstration of who I am or want to be?"

Circumstances and conviction make it difficult for many teachers to commit to student self-assessment. Fortunately, the spectrum of approaches to SDL is matched by a spectrum of approaches to assessment. Teachers can grade all student work. In most self-managed learning programs, students have to pass a test of the material in each learning guide with at least 80 percent before they move to the next guide. Teachers can also include student self-assessment as part of their approach to evaluation, or they can include self-assessment on certain activities for a certain percentage of a course grade. Nevertheless, cross-grade testing, ranking, grading, and reporting exclude students from the assessment process, make most students relative failures, enforce mass curriculum rather than cultivating individual programs, and contribute very little to students' understanding about their learning. In full self-assessment, students of SDL in senior grades work hard to create their own—and the only—transcript of achievements that they will take from high school and present to colleges for admission committee review or to potential employers when it is appropriate. Transcripts focus students on doing their best work to represent themselves. SDL is about making every student successful.

From the beginning of any SDL course or program, students should be learning to think about and assess the whole learning sequence: what they have chosen to learn, the process they are following to complete the tasks they have chosen, the success with which they are applying their energies to the tasks, and the quality of the results they achieved. The criteria of success, just like the tasks that they are pursuing, vary from student to student. What is important is that the student establish the criteria for a successful outcome before the work begins. This can be done in a general way by providing the student with a list of the characteristics of a successful performance in SDL as a guide, or by providing rubrics of poor, satisfactory, and outstanding work so that students can see what performance at different levels of success looks like. A successful performance can also be defined by students in their learning proposals or contracts and negotiated with the teacher. The key is that both parties must know and agree to the level of performance involved in the activity and that both will be able to recognize it when it occurs. The criteria are also usually implicit in the demonstration that the student cites in his or her plans and agrees to achieve. If flying solo is the demonstration activity, accomplishing it is also the criterion for success. The basis for assessing SDL activities is knowing from the beginning what the student will do, by what date, and how well. It also means defining that fine line of challenge where students have to struggle for success but where success is an attainable expectation.

Students can also benefit from learning to monitor and improve their own work and study habits. If they establish specific goals with time lines for an evening, a day, or a week and then measure their results and compare them with their expectations, they will quickly see whether they are performing well. Show them how to identify impediments to their efficiency and competence and how to correct them. Self-observation and honest assessment are critical for the pursuit of excellence in SDL.

Many approaches are available to ensure that students complete their work to the established criteria and are learning to assess the process as well as the product.

Promoting Student Self-Assessment

A program designed to teach students to be self-directed must engage them in the ongoing assessment of their work. In TDL, the emphasis is on results: scores on tests of content mastery. In SDL, students learn to assess the importance of what they have accomplished and much more, including these aspects of learning:

- My attitudes as a learner. How focused was I? How disciplined? How strategic? How committed?

- My approaches to the task. How skillful did I become? How effective was the approach I took? How organized was I?

- My ability to solve problems. How well did I identify difficulties? Consider alternatives? Develop solutions?

- My success. How good was the job I did? Did I meet my goals? My criteria for success? Can I see ways for me to improve this work?

Teachers can prepare students in a number of ways to deal with these questions:

- Present models of varying quality for students to assess—essays, videos, poems, reports, and performances. Discuss with students the nature of quality and the criteria for excellence, then, together with students, assess the models and organize them from poor to excellent.

- Present aspects of learning—the appropriateness of their goals, the effectiveness of their plans, and the success of their study and work strategies—as topics for students to discuss in their journals regularly, especially with reference to their current activities. In SDL, learning means improving in all dimensions of the process, as well as in the products produced.

- Ask students to include their assessment of both their work and their results, along with the products that they submit or present. The teacher can then respond not only to the work but also to the process or procedure the students employed.

- Teach students how to monitor and improve their own work patterns, showing them how to set goals for an hour, day, or week and then examining how much of their expectations they achieved. Then teachers can show the students how to identify and remove impediments and how to recognize and enhance strengths. Self-observation, honest assessment, and the adoption of alternatives are essential for successful SDL.

- When students demonstrate their achievements, ask them to include assessments of their feelings, their process, and their performance or product.

- Teach students in support groups how to assess their own performances and learn how to comment constructively on the work of others.

Assessment is the key to improvement. It is learning. By improving attitudes and process as well as the product of any learning enterprise, students are becoming equipped to pursue excellence.

Assessing General Skills

The simplest way to present a full description of expectations is the Personal Performance Profile, a list of the competencies that the student is expected to acquire during the SDL program (see Exhibit 8.1). It includes skills, attitudes, and achievements. It can be used as a self-rating instrument by students and as a vehicle for teachers to give students feedback. If both the student and the teacher fill out the profile, they can use it during conferences as information for discussions of progress and goals for the future. In these ways, it helps students to guide their efforts as well as to assess their success. Some students place the profile in their portfolios; others use it as a guide for organizing the transcript in which they summarize their achievements for graduation.

The example in Exhibit 8.1 lists the skills, attitudes, and general achievements central to an SDL program. The phases refer to sections of a course, and the numbers are ratings that teachers can give to students and students can give to themselves. You can create your own profile or adapt this one to include your list of the course outcomes, expectations, or competencies that students are expected to achieve. At Jefferson County Open, for example, students pursue twenty-seven expectations, which are broad statements of outcome topics that students rewrite as specific personal goals. For the general expectation that students "will become skilled at numeracy," for example, some students will take the math courses offered, some will use Internet programs, some may take on practical tasks such as managing the books for a family business, and others may take math courses at a nearby college.

Providing space at the back or end of the profile for comments at different times throughout the course or program encourages students and teachers to interpret what the ratings suggest as guidance for future progress and as a focus for conferences between them. Exhibit 8.2, for example, shows a student's comments on various items of the profile in Exhibit 8.1 for the first assessment period. Use as many assessment techniques as possible to provide the ongoing feedback students need to stay on track and to check their progress.

Assessing Coursework

Course outcomes define what the student must learn (for example, "Explain the dynamics of our solar system"). The task of assessment is to determine how well students achieve the outcomes. In TDL, the teacher

EXHIBIT 8.1

Personal Performance Profile

Self-rate on a scale from 10 (very capable) to 1 (minimal performance).

Attribute	Program Phase			
	1	2	3	4
Understands self-management and pursues it	2			
Recognizes strengths; works to overcome limitations	2			
Sets clear, appropriate, workable goals	6			
Exhibits sense of direction, clarity, commitment	6			
Designs plans that lead to achievement of goals	6			
Plans using a range of learning resources and activities	8			
Is developing a productive personal learning style	6			
Chooses personally challenging activities	8			
Is positive; approaches tasks confidently	6			
Organizes and uses time efficiently	2			
Secures needed resources independently	4			
Solves problems; overcomes obstacles and setbacks that arise in projects	4			
Exhibits drive and determination in the pursuit of goals	4			
Measures and reports on progress	6			
Is a cooperative and contributing group member	8			
Interacts with others responsibly	8			
Identifies needed skills; creates programs for learning them	2			
Completes projects and demonstrates achievement effectively	0			
Performs with increasing skill and effectiveness	2			
Is creating a coherent sense of meaning and a thoughtful worldview	—			
Examines self and makes changes	—			
Understands and can apply processes	6			
Verbalizes and demonstrates worthy values	2			
Demonstrates and celebrates with pride and pleasure	—			
Is developing a vision of a desirable future	2			

Source: *Reproduced with permission from Personal Power Press International, Inc.*

assesses students' achievement by administering tests (with questions like, "Describe and explain planet rotation and revolution"). In SDL, students assess their own achievement ("I built a model of the solar system and demonstrated its dynamics to the class") and the process by which it was attained. Self-assessment and self-correction are important elements of self-directed learning. Learning how to learn involves assessing and improving the process one follows in order to learn.

EXHIBIT 8.2

Student Comments on the Personal Performance Profile, Initial Assessment

Item Numbers	Comment
6, 7, 8	I feel good about the goals I picked and a lot of ways I'm going after them.
15, 16	I never worked in groups before. I'm doing okay. Feels good.
1, 2, 10	Looks like I need organization. That's what everyone says.
17, 19, 23, 25	I guess I don't think ahead any more than I have to.

Rubrics and Performance Criteria

Measurement of student progress should be conducted in a way that involves students and is a part of the learning process. One way of doing that is to state the requirements specifically and clearly. John Holt (1964) said that "most students clearly understand the teacher's expectations only when they fail to meet them." Making expectations clear from the beginning of the course, the unit, or the day helps students to focus, direct their energies, and learn. It also enables students to be partners in the process—partners who know where the activities are going and why. Stating course outcomes is the best way to make expectations clear from the beginning. The clear statement of expectations enables students to participate in evaluation and learn from it.

If circumstances require the teacher and students to achieve specified performance standards, these should also be declared so that students can be involved in preparing themselves for success on the grade, school, or district tests that they will take. Teachers can clarify the standards by providing rubrics that illustrate levels of performance and summaries of criteria that identify the features of excellence.

At Francis W. Parker Charter Essential School in Devens, Massachusetts, for example, the focus is on twelve basic skill areas:

Reading

Writing

Oral presentation

Artistic expression

Research

Scientific investigation

Spanish language

Mathematical problem solving and communication

Listening

Systems thinking

Technology

Wellness

Students study integrated domains: Arts and Humanities (which encompasses history, philosophy, social sciences, literature, and the expressive arts and which includes a Spanish team), Mathematics, Science, Technology, and Wellness. Students in multiage groups progress through three divisions to graduation, with each division representing roughly two years of traditional schooling (for example, division 1 represents grades 7 and 8). There are no grades; students progress and graduate on the basis of their exhibited work. Students move to a higher division by organizing what is called a gateway portfolio for presentation to a small audience of advisers, teachers, parents, peers, and other members of the community. Students keep portfolios of their best work and select from them for their gateway presentation. They also include a letter they have written reflecting on their progress over the two-year cycle. The presentation is preserved on videotape, and as the program description states, "we honor it by our presence and congratulatory rituals."

Parker follows an inquiry-based curriculum and each year addresses a new schoolwide "essential question" such as, "What is community?" "What are the patterns?" and "What is change?" At the end of every year, students assemble a portfolio that displays the progress they have achieved in the twelve essential skill areas during their studies. Assessment of performance in the skills—whether by students, teachers, parents, or others—is guided by two instruments: the Holistic Rubric, which outlines a continuum of progress for the skill, and the Criteria for Excellence, which outlines specifically what students can do when they have achieved excellence in the skill. Exhibit 8.3 shows the Holistic Rubric for the Scientific Investigation skill, which specifies four basic levels of progress. There are no grades, only these guides for students as they draw up their individual plans and to students and all other interested parties as they assess their progress.

EXHIBIT 8.3

Holistic Rubric for the Scientific Investigation Skill

Just Beginning
- You show limited understanding of the question you are investigating.
- Your hypothesis cannot be tested with your plan, or you have no plan for testing it.
- Your physical observations are inaccurate or not recorded in a useful way.
- You have not considered alternative explanations for what you observe or shown logical reasoning in drawing your conclusion.
- You do not verify your results or identify sources of possible error or bias.
- Your explanation of your conclusions does not use accurate math-science vocabulary or visual representations, or it is unclear to the audience.
- You conduct the investigation but do not comment about what it might mean.
- You do not complete the investigation, or you show no evidence of reflecting on your process and thinking.

EXHIBIT 8.3 (continued)

Approaches Division 1 Standards
- You show some understanding of the question you are investigating.
- You present a testable hypothesis, but your plan for testing it is incomplete.
- Your physical observations are incomplete or imprecise.
- You present alternative explanations for what you observe, but your reasoning is only partly correct in drawing conclusions.
- You try to verify your results, but you miss sources of possible error or bias.
- Your explanation of your conclusions correctly uses some math-science vocabulary or visual representations.
- You conduct the investigation and make some comments about what it might mean.
- You attempted most of the investigation, and you show some evidence of reflecting on your process and thinking.

Meets Division 1 Standards ("Yes, and ..." "Yes, but ...")
- You understand the question you are investigating.
- You present a hypothesis and a workable plan for testing it.
- Your physical observations are complete and accurate.
- You present alternative explanations for what you observe, and your conclusions suggest logical reasoning, but that reasoning is not clearly explained.
- You try to verify your results and identify at least one possible source of error and bias.
- Your explanation of your conclusions correctly uses appropriate math-science vocabulary and visual representations.
- You conduct the investigation and connect your conclusion to other ideas you know about or to a real-world use.
- You attempted the entire investigation, and you show some evidence of reflecting on your process and thinking.

Exceeds Division 1 Standards ("Yes!")
- You understand the question you are investigating and identify the variables or special factors that may affect your investigation before starting.
- You present a hypothesis and an efficient or sophisticated plan for testing it.
- Your physical observations are extensive, precise, and sustained.
- You present alternative explanations for what you observe, and you clearly explain the reasons for your logical conclusions.
- You verify your results and identify several possible sources of error and bias.
- Your explanation of your conclusions uses sophisticated math-science vocabulary and effective visual representations.
- You conduct the investigation and connect your conclusion to other ideas you know about or to a real-world use.
- You attempted more than the required investigation, and you reflect thoughtfully on your process and thinking.

Source: *Reproduced with permission from Francis W. Parker Charter Essential School, Devens, Massachusetts.*

The Criteria for Excellence in Scientific Investigation (see Exhibit 8.4) outline exactly what students will be able to do when their performance is outstanding. Although the standards and progressions remain stable from grades 7 through 12, students are expected to address more difficult tasks, work more independently, and become more aware of the meaning of their own work and the work of others.

Testing Outcome Achievement

Teachers always have the alternative of testing student achievement. They can also balance teacher-made tests with student-directed methods of proving achievement. Students working through a series of learning packages

---

EXHIBIT 8.4

Criteria for Excellence: Scientific Investigation

Framing the Question

- You understand or come up with the question to investigate.
- You collect information and ideas about your question.
- You identify the variables or special factors that may affect your investigation.

Approach: How You Conduct the Investigation

- You come up with a hypothesis.
- You make a plan for testing the hypothesis.
- You identify and use appropriate scientific equipment.
- You make and record physical observations.

Reasoning: How You Evaluate What You Find

- You consider alternative explanations for what you observe.
- You use evidence to draw a logical conclusion.
- You identify possible sources of error and bias in the investigation.
- You verify the results of the investigation.
- You revise your explanation if necessary.

Communicating What You Find

- You explain your ideas and procedures to others in a form they can understand.
- You use correct mathematical and scientific vocabulary, equations, or notations to explain your ideas.
- You use graphs, tables, charts, models, diagrams, or drawings to represent your findings.

So What: Outcomes of Your Investigation

- You connect your ideas to other ideas in math or science or to a real-world use.
- You use data to respond to questions or comments from others.
- You reflect on your own scientific process and thinking.

What You Try

- You attempt the entire investigation process or go beyond it to do more.

Source: *Reproduced with permission from Francis W. Parker Charter Essential School, Devens, Massachusetts.*

---

or guides usually have to prove that they have learned the content of one guide before they can proceed to the next. This can be done in a number of ways. They can take a test, hand in a project, converse with a teacher or a teacher substitute, make a presentation to the teacher or the class, or supply evidence—a certificate or letter, for example—to prove their achievement in another location.

The mastery of the learning guide dealing with volcanic action, for instance, might be tested by answering a series of multiple-choice questions, taking a brief oral exam, presenting a model of volcanic action, identifying volcanic stones and formations, or writing a paper on volcanism. At Thomas Haney, for example, many teachers make the tests for learning guide completion at the senior level duplicate as closely as possible the tests that students will have to answer on their scholarship exams required and set by the provincial governments in Canada.

Evaluating Projects and Assignments

When students propose an activity, they can also propose a way to assess their achievement. On action contracts, for example, students can establish a baseline performance, which is a description or demonstration of how well they can perform in the proposed activity before they begin. Sometimes it is difficult to define a baseline performance. One student, for example, had never cooked before. Her baseline was, "No knowledge of cooking, no experience of cooking (except toast), no ability to cook." Sometimes the baseline can be described only in general terms: "We had a unit on Mexico last year. I've heard folks talking about NAFTA at dinner, and I read up about it to see if it was worth doing this project on trade." Sometimes the baseline can be captured on audiotape or videotape, for example, in a recording of a performance on a musical instrument, speaking a foreign language, or making an oral presentation. The baseline can often be measured with a score on tests, a score in an athletic competition, or the number of things done in a certain time (for example, the number of bushels harvested in a day). Ingenuity is required, and students will find a way.

Three Ways to Use Alumni in Assessment

- Use the work of former students to show the class how others have handled evaluation.

- Bring former students back to your class to talk about their experience with evaluation and how

they made it work. Students will ask them questions they might hesitate to ask the teacher.

- Invite graduates of the program to sit on advisory committees so they can contribute their experience to students in process.

Students can then measure progress against this baseline. It is helpful to ask students to describe an unsatisfactory, an ordinary, and an excellent performance. Knowing what "unsatisfactory" or "minimal" looks like eliminates it as an alternative; describing a satisfactory, ordinary, or acceptable outcome often eliminates it too, but it is a safe fallback position. Excellence, as described by students for themselves, is what they work to achieve. In consulting on proposals, make sure that students do not trivialize performance ("I will learn to calculate area") or think impossibly broadly ("I will apply chaos theory to history"). Of course, for some students, calculating area *is* a challenge, and some students are capable of applying chaos theory. Do not try to equalize the challenges in a class; judge if the challenge is the right stretch for the individual. Costanza is an eleventh grader beginning her graduation passage in "practical applications." She is very interested in business, and especially in opening her own store. This is the assessment section of her learning agreement:

> Baseline: I know the basic facts about this country and Mexico; I know what NAFTA is and the general idea of trade agreements.
>
> Satisfactory: I learn how trade operates between the US and Mexico and make charts for a class presentation. I show how it works.
>
> Excellent: I find a source for Mexican leather goods. I do all the paperwork to import them for sale in my store. I display the import forms. I show how it all fits into NAFTA and other trade agreements about such goods.

Proposals or contracts may be evaluated by students' demonstrations and explanations of their achievements. Presenting a first aid certificate, a pilot's license, or college course grades speaks for itself. Others may be assessed through written reports and still others by appropriate testing.

Costanza, the student interested in business, for example, felt that she had a great experience in her graduation passage but did not have something like a successful working store to demonstrate her success. There was no available test to write and show what she had learned. Her evaluation took the form of a report, supported by documents, about her personal performance, what she accomplished, and the level of achievement that her work represented. Her discussion about organization led to her assessment of her achievement:

> My vision is to start my own leather goods store after I graduate and work in business for a while. I'll import (I found a Mexican supplier), but I'm artistic. I'm going to start making simple things like belts, until I learn how to do more. This contract prepared me. I know exactly what to do to import product, get a license and

insurance, set up my store and keep my books. With my dad's help
I may rent a store he found on the island where we go for summer
holidays and do a test run of my plan. I think I did a lot more than
my excellence statement required.

Within the restrictions that your teaching situation places on you, find
the way to assess student progress that most involves students in self-evaluation, an approach that is individual and that motivates and guides student effort.

Portfolios for Personal Learning

The portfolio is an effective and appropriate means of measuring the success of students in SDL. Prepared by the student, it contains the student's best work and proof of achievements away from the classroom. The portfolio is the basis for assessment at the end of a course or program and at graduation. In it, the student collects items such as the following:

- Products from assignments in coursework and test results, such as letters, essays, reports, drawings, photographs, and videos

- Written products, such as essays, stories, songs, reports on activities, research, campaigns (for the environment, for instance), and publications

- Photographs, drawings, tapes, or copies of creative work, such as paintings, sculptures, jewelry, designs of buildings, clothes, recordings, and any other imaginative products

- Pictures of such work as constructions, models, performances, inventions, trips, and creative products of all kinds, such as paintings, jewelry, architectural designs, advertisements, and pottery

- Proof of achievement in nonschool studies and activities: report cards, certificates, and awards

- Letters of validation: reports by observers, other teachers, sponsors, employers, mentors, and other informants

- A personal report by the student describing what she or he learned

A portfolio can be both a powerful part of the learning process and a suitable instrument for assessment. It gains power by focusing student attention on building a body of evidence that is as impressive as possible. To make the most of this drive, introduce the portfolio early, and present it as the opportunity for students to show what they can do without limits. It is a suitable instrument for assessment because it permits students to display their accomplishments in the most advantageous way possible. They become advocates for their own learning. Some teachers and some institutions enhance this process by encouraging students to upgrade their portfolios by improving the items in them—by rewriting essays, for example—as much as they wish.

In the portfolio-building process, they are preparing the documents they will present to colleges and universities they wish to attend. One school has a counselor who contacts the institutions students apply to and paves the way for their applications. Other institutions have committees prepared to consider portfolios if they are accompanied by Scholastic Aptitude Test scores. Few other approaches to final assessment are more appropriate for SDL programs. Evaluation is, first of all, another way to learn.

Students usually include a summary of their activities and a personal assessment of themselves, their performance, and their achievements. Their assessment is supported by products and proofs or validations of their activities and successes. In their senior year, the portfolio takes on a special importance. It is the most impressive possible accumulation of achievements as a demonstration—to teachers, colleges, or employers—of who they are and what they can do.

Passage and Graduation Criteria

Teachers in different situations require different ways to establish criteria for the assessment of the diverse activities that contribute to students' achieving graduation. To put it simply, SDL assessment is student self-assessment, but if teachers must test and grade, they must. But there are alternatives. Students preparing for graduation are usually involved in different kinds of activities: meeting course requirements (usually in basic subjects such as math, science, English, and history), achieving competencies (such as computer proficiency, small group leadership, public presentations, and excellence in a field of choice), and completing passages or challenges (such as adventure, career, inquiry, and service work). Each of these can be assessed for graduation in a different way. Course requirements, reduced to core essentials, may be taught in classes, offered on-line, presented in packages, or listed as outcomes that students must achieve. These can be tested and graded conventionally.

Competencies

Competencies may be regarded as course outcomes that students achieve by following their own plans. Those plans, negotiated with a teacher, include a description of achievement and the criteria by which it can be judged. Again, the student performance can be graded, or the grade can be negotiated, but a great deal of the educational value of the activity is lost when the assessment is taken out of the hands of the student. To remain true to the process, the student's assessment should stand.

The critical issue is whether the student's performance merits the assessment it receives. The teacher's concern is to ensure that students see their performances realistically, without seeing success as failure or failure as success. When the student, the teacher, or both establish the criteria for different levels of success before the learning activity begins, they have a clear reference for assessment when the activity is over. Often the activity, the competency, and the criteria are one; doing it is complete in itself: Elizabeth conducts successful experiments in crystal formation; Jack climbs Mount Rainier; Kate gets out of bed into her wheelchair, goes down the elevator, and for the first time reaches the library and checks out a book; Bill researches high-density TV in the library and the Internet and then writes a report; Jean gets a lifesaving certificate and a job as lifeguard. Who gets the A? The question is irrelevant and can be destructive. Each of these students set goals, described achievement, and then got the job done. All must receive the affirmation they deserve.

Passages

Passages are activities in which students challenge themselves to the most demanding possible performance in the fields assigned. Students settle on the criteria as part of the proposals they present and negotiate. They often work on their six passages—logical inquiry, practical application, career focus, creativity, adventure, and service—over the final two years of school, using both in-school and out-of-school time. The criteria that students establish are the criteria by which the passages should be evaluated, and evaluated by the student. The teacher is the student's advocate who does everything possible to ensure that the student achieves the greatest possible success.

Graduation Transcripts

The transcript is a document submitted for graduation and supported by the master portfolio in which students collect their best work, that is, the work that presents them to the greatest advantage. It is a prepared booklet in which students state why they have earned the right to graduate and then support their case with documentation.

The transcript is the student's passport from school to college or work. It is a book of from thirty to fifty pages, as impressive as possible in content and design, that the student can take, as architects and artists take their portfolios, for submission to admissions officers and employers. It contains many items from the portfolio to validate the learning experiences they have collected to meet the requirements of graduation. Many students go far beyond what is required and create impressive dossiers of achievement. Building a powerful transcript becomes an overarching goal for many students.

Here is a brief list of the items found in a selection of transcripts from Saint Paul Open in Saint Paul, Minnesota, and Jefferson County Open:

- A contents page
- A summary and commentary on student achievements
- A plan for the future
- Letters of validation for achievement in a variety of academic and practical activities, ranging from validation of employment-seeking skills to completion of a university-level course in calculus
- Certificates of participation, completion, and excellence in everything from student government to professional theater and Outward Bound Mountain School
- Grade sheets from open school, other school, and college and university courses, and programs at special institutes in everything from playing jazz to developing computer programs
- A summary of all courses, institutes, service activities, and other achievements
- A list of books that the student read during the last two years of school
- A list of the student's advisory committee members (with space for signatures of approval), which includes a counselor, a program coordinator, an adviser, parents, a student, and a program graduate
- Photographs, drawings, and quotations such as the following, which could be posters on any SDL classroom wall: "'A ship in harbor is safe, but that is not what ships are built for,'—William Shedd"

Content of Letters of Validation

Letters of validation are in memo form and contain the following information:

- The date
- The competency to be validated
- The validator's name, position, title, and a brief statement of background
- A specific outline of what the student did
- The validator's observations about what the student learned and the level of performance she or he achieved
- The validator's full signature

The activity summary for Renata Tremblay (see Exhibit 8.5), a student at Saint Paul Open School, gives a snapshot of this twelfth grader's high school experience. Notice how her work is balanced between coursework and independent fieldwork. The headings are for required areas of activity. Exhibit 8.6 contains samples from the validation letters she collected. When the doctor at the naturopathic clinic was unable to write a comprehensive

---

EXHIBIT 8.5

A Twelfth Grader's Course and Activity List

Arts and Music
African Drum Making—Evenstar School
Independent study—poetry performance
Independent study—architectural photography
Independent study—visual examination of prison culture
Politics and photography—Open School

English
English composition—College of St. Catherine
Independent study—video communication
Independent study—women in literature
Mythology—Open School
Poetry—Open School
Poetry—Second Foundation School
Revolutions in Literature—Open School
University of Minnesota Writing Study

Health Sciences
Acupressure and Massage—Open University
Aromatherapy—Evenstar School
Emergency 911—St. Paul Technical College
Homeopathy—Open University
Independent study—naturopathic medicine
Independent study—nutrition and personal health
Independent study—reproductive rights of mentally retarded women
Medicinal Herbalism—Evenstar School

Industrial Arts and Home Economics
Independent study—living spaces for the disabled
Independent study—construction of adventure course

Mathematics
Algebra II with trigonometry
Geometry
Independent study—Shape and space; math in art

(continued)

EXHIBIT 8.5 (continued)

Physical Education

Independent study—Boundary Waters Canoe Area Wilderness trips

Independent study—backpacking Superior View Trail

Independent study—desert backpacking

Independent study—flat water canoeing and portaging

Independent study—mountain backpacking

Independent study—white water canoeing

Sciences

Chemistry

Genetics

Genetics and Ethics

Independent study—computer science

Independent study—desert ecosystems

Independent study—edible plants

Independent study—trees and plants of northern Minnesota

Source: *Reproduced with permission from Saint Paul Open School, St. Paul, Minnesota.*

---

letter, Renata wrote him a thank-you letter in which she documented everything she did, and he signed a copy of it.

Demonstrations, Celebrations, and Conferences

Demonstrations

Demonstrations are exhibitions of work, the presentation of proofs such as certificates and letters, and performances by students to teachers and others that show as conclusively as possible that they have completed the work that they proposed. It is an opportunity for students to "strut their stuff" in the best and most convincing ways that they can devise. Demonstrations can occur at the end of a project, a course, a year, or a program division, or at graduation. They are always presented by the student to an audience that may include teachers, other students, parents, and other adults, especially those who have been involved in the student's activities. They may include such items as the following:

- Exhibitions of work, including items from the student's portfolio

- Letters about the student's work at out-of-class sites

- Grades of courses taken at other institutions or on-line, including teachers' comments

- Certificates for such activities as lifeguarding or lifesaving and awards of achievement or excellence

EXHIBIT 8.6

Selections from Validation Letters

Re: Request for Cultural Awareness Validation

I highly recommend that Ms. Renata Tremblay be most favorably considered by the committee for credit for her work toward the Native American Cultural Awareness Validation. Renata has excellently exhibited an eagerness to seek out a wide variety of sources and produced a tremendous effort at thorough research in her study of Native American culture. Not only did she bring a strong commitment for excellence to the task she had to accomplish, she also brought a positive attitude and firm and unyielding belief in the justness and necessity behind such an inquiry. The insights she has gained into American Indian culture are extremely impressive to me.

Re: Current Issues Validation

I am writing to validate Renata Tremblay's current issues competencies as demonstrated through her valuable participation as a member of the Minnesota Fellowship of Reconciliation.

Renata is among the most active members of the MN FOR. In addition to monthly two-hour meetings, Renata has twice been to week-long national leadership training conferences, one in Washington, D.C., and another in Santa Cruz, California. Her enthusiasm for both experiences bubbles forth with little prompting. National FOR officers have reported that Renata was a model participant, hard working, and engaged. Activities included policy study and organizing for handgun reform and to combat racism.

Renata has been active on a local level as well. She is involved in campus organizing for peace and justice with area students. This fall the focus will be on a comprehensive ban of the production and distribution of anti-personnel landmines. She has met several Bosnian student refugees sponsored locally by the MN FOR and may involve them in area student workshops. And she gave moving and articulate testimony on the presence of violence in her life as a member of a panel of local and international youth speaking last fall for the statewide annual conference.

Re: Validation for Coherent Communication, Part A

Renata, it is with great pleasure that I grant you validation in the area of Coherent Communication, Part A. Your participation in our writing course has been in all ways absolutely stellar. You exemplify the kind of success that is possible with unyielding effort and enthusiasm. To say that your writing has truly improved would be putting things far too lightly. You have been the consummate writer, group member, and pursuer of knowledge. I offer you my enthusiastic congratulations on a fine, fine success.

Re: Service to the Community Validation

I am pleased to validate Renata in the area of Service to the Community. Whenever I have had the opportunity to work with Renata, she has been energetic and dedicated. I am confident Renata competently met and exceeded the requirements for this validation.

Source: *Reproduced with permission from Saint Paul Open School, St. Paul, Minnesota.*

- Videotapes or photographs of work in the field

- Creative products, such as paintings, poems, publications, films, plays, or performances

- Practical products, such as constructions, inventions, scientific data or other research, computer programs, apparatus, or models

- Performances, such as acting, singing, athletics, yoga, teaching, displays of competence in a foreign language, or reenactments of activities

- Testimonials (written, taped, or in person) from people helped or people the student worked with or informed observers

- In-school coursework, including notes, essays, charts, tests, and projects

- Student presentation about achievements, learning experiences, and the personal significance and value of these achievements and experiences

Demonstrations may include any of these items or any others that students may devise to show their achievements to their best advantage. Such performances require and display competence in a number of skills themselves, such as organization, oral presentation, and creativity. Everything possible should be done to support students in their preparation. One important outcome is their greater confidence in their work and their ability to face an audience successfully. Students put themselves at risk in these presentations, and success is essential.

Demonstration is an important learning experience in itself. Anticipate emotion if a student's experiences have been dramatic. SDL often involves struggle with one's self as well as with achievement, and as students talk about the difficulties they faced and overcame, they may experience strong feelings. Be sure that students are prepared—that they have success to report and the skill to do it well. Demonstration is the basis for celebration. In such circumstances their expression of feelings will be positive rather than problematical.

Costanza completed her walkabout program, which focused on her interests in business, her Mexican heritage, and her relationship with her Malaysian stepmother. At her graduation demonstration, she reported on her academic accomplishments and her work meeting six challenges:

- Adventure Challenge: Exploring her own cultural background. American born, she knew little of her Mexican father's culture and her stepmother's Malaysian heritage. Her inner quest was to understand her stepmother's background and establish a better relationship with her. She studied both Mexico and Malaysia and spent time in both local communities, including working in a Malaysian restaurant.

- Creative Challenge: Creating jewelry. With her uncle's help, she arranged an apprenticeship with a Mexican jeweler and produced six pieces of jewelry, which were on display.

- Career Challenge: Exploring a career in business like her father, a furniture dealer. She shadowed her father to learn the basics of buying, displaying, selling, and bookkeeping. Then she attended a sales seminar, explored the requirements for a degree in commerce at a local university, and wrote a report on pursuing a career in retail.

- Practical Application Challenge: Cooking, especially Mexican and Malaysian food. Both of her parents cooked, so she learned from them. Cooking with her stepmother was part of her strategy in meeting her Adventure Challenge. She showed pictures of the dinner she cooked for her greater family—sixteen people.

- Logical Inquiry Challenge: A study of trade relationships, especially those between the United States and Mexico. With the idea of importing products from Mexico suggested by her adviser, she read about existing trade agreements and then approached the Mexican Trade Office as if she were importing products. With the assistance of that office, she followed all of the steps to import Mexican leather goods for sale. She displayed a chart showing these steps and another showing the principles of the North American Free Trade Agreement and how they would affect her transactions.

- Service Challenge: Helping Mexican immigrant children to adjust to school. She realized that many adolescent immigrants were having difficulties, so she placed a notice on the school bulletin board and had two replies, which led to eight more. She held meetings at school to discuss problems, offered individual counseling, and met with parents. One student attended her demonstration to speak about the service she provided.

In Costanza's audience were most of her advisory group, her adviser, her father and three other family members, several other students, two drop-by teachers, and a surprise visitor from the Mexican embassy. She spoke briefly about her creativity and service challenges and introduced a student from her service group. Most of her report dealt with her decision to pursue a career in commerce and her Adventure Challenge. Her project began badly. Her fierce stepmother, unskilled in English, had resisted her first initiatives. Costanza became emotional describing the breakthrough around cooking. Her stepmother thought she was lazy and unappreciative, but over the family stove, cooking together, they began to talk. Costanza was so moved by the memory, she could hardly report what her stepmother said so affectionately about her at the family meal that she cooked and served. Learning "to understand and reach out instead of reacting and shutting down" was the single most important thing she said that she learned in all that she did. When she finished, she answered questions and heard some admiring testimony from her peers and teachers. Her adviser presented her graduation certificate, and her father proudly embraced her. The celebration had begun.

Celebrations

In SDL, students strive for ambitious attainments; they struggle, take risks, fall down, and get up again to keep going as far as they can. They are learning and changing. Within the class, everyone knows what is happening and has happened to their peers; they have helped, comforted, and advised each other. The ideal time for students to celebrate is when they know this history, they have seen the demonstrations of what each of them has accomplished with the guidance of their teachers, and they have felt the collective energy of the class. Celebration is the individual expression of pleasure and relief at having achieved success—including the risky demonstrations they have just completed—combined with their collective feeling as a learning community that they have made a leap forward together. Teachers should make time for it, acknowledge it, and organize or help students organize some celebratory festivity to express it. Celebrate those who achieved and those who helped and supported them with ceremony—words, accolades, stories, and humor.

Celebrations may include food and drink, a special trip or event, and a simple ritual. The celebration affirms individuals, builds group spirit, and can be a profound and memorable part of assessment and the SDL experience. It occurs whenever there is demonstration or completion during the year, when the year ends and work is done, and especially at graduation, when the celebration of achievement becomes the celebration of transition to adulthood as well.

Conferences

Conferences—meetings between individual students, their teachers, and possibly others—can include the following:

- Planning conferences: Students present proposals for SDL activities to teachers or meet to report progress and discuss problems.

- Trouble-shooting conferences: Teachers meet with students who are experiencing or causing problems.

- Report-time conferences: At report time, SDL students often present their achievements to their parents and other interested parties.

Teachers can assess progress and achievement by holding regular conferences with each student during the course or program and a final conference at the end of it. Scheduled in-process conferences provide intermediate goals for students to aim at and an opportunity for the teacher to check progress and guide further effort and activities. Whenever possible, the conferences should be student led. Parent support for the program is important, and parents—or their substitutes—can be very helpful in encouraging students and helping with the program in many ways. For those reasons, consider inviting them to some conferences during the course or program and especially to the final assessment conference. Their participation not only keeps them informed and supportive, but also increases the significance of the conference for students.

In conferences they lead, students present their best work and describe what they have learned in a course or in all of their activities during a program period. By presenting to a smaller group—teachers and parents—they have an opportunity to practice the skills they will need for their major presentations at graduation, and teachers have an opportunity to guide that development.

Two, three, or even four final assessment conferences can be run simultaneously, with the teacher moving from one to the other. Allowing about thirty minutes for each conference period, a class of twenty or more can be processed comfortably in an afternoon and evening. Such presentations are highly motivating for students.

• • •

All of these methods of assessment involve students in assessing themselves and their work. The result is that students not only work toward both a public and a private vision of success, they learn to evaluate and improve their progress on those paths as well. With such methods, all students can legitimately hope to excel, to leap beyond their existing level of performance; even if they do not leap to the greatest height, they can still leap far from where they were. The task of every SDL teacher is to assemble a system of assessment that teaches students how to be more thoughtfully self-directing and equips them with the attitudes and tools to continue learning in the years ahead.

Chapter 9

Pursuing a Path of Excellence

WE HAVE COVERED a lot of ground and probed deeply into the nature and practice of SDL, an educational approach in which students learn to complete the requirements of their courses independently and go beyond these requirements to pursue their own challenging goals (see the summary in Exhibit 9.1). Through this process, they not only become skilled in managing the educational enterprise, they also produce astonishing results, and in the fires of their struggles, they are tempered into young men and women of accomplishment and character. Teachers and administrators become justifiably proud of what they have made possible together. In these final pages, we consider what teachers and administrators can do to establish an SDL program and why that initiative is an important step to take.

The Teacher Is the Key Person

The key person in the development of SDL courses, programs, and schools is the teacher. Developments in schooling are often determined by specialists and authorities who choose the outcomes, design the curriculum, select the textbooks and other materials, and then assign the program to teachers as a complete package, often embedded in a testing program to ensure that teachers and schools are producing the prescribed results. This top-down model may be suitable for the delivery of a single program for all students, but it is unsuitable for SDL, a program in which each student is developing individually, following a personal program in a special learning relationship with teachers and other students. SDL is a grassroots program that emerges from groups of teachers committed to creating the best possible program for the successful education of each student.

EXHIBIT 9.1

Teaching SDL: A Summary

Prepare Your Course
- Declare the required outcomes of your course.
- Expand the learning options available to students.
- Create an open, supportive classroom environment.
- Choose the level of self-direction that you will seek.
- Plan how you will introduce your class to SDL.

Create Learning Episodes
- Establish experiences that provoke learning and wonder.
- Conduct investigations that lead to deeper understanding.
- Organize student performances of productivity.
- Teach the portable skills that episodes require.
- Teach the processes required to get things done.
- Teach perspective by placing activities in a systems framework.

Negotiate Student Contracts
- Establish a procedure students use to propose SDL activities.
- Organize advisory and support groups.
- Meet with students to negotiate their proposals or contracts.
- Monitor student progress on their contracts; intervene as required.
- Provide special instruction for students who need it.

Motivate Students to Motivate Themselves
- Teach students to find their own interests and set their own goals.
- Teach students to charge their goals with value.
- Teach students to organize a system of feedback on performance.
- Build patterns of success for students; build self-efficacy.

Teach Students How to Assess and Prove Their Own Progress
- Teach students a process of ongoing assessment of performance and progress.
- Teach students to regulate and improve their own process and performance.
- Teach students to measure performance beyond an established baseline.
- Teach students to build a strong portfolio and an impressive transcript of their accomplishments.
- Create regular opportunities for students to demonstrate their achievements.

The perfect medium for teachers preparing to teach SDL is provided by SDL itself. The right teacher for self-directed learning is the self-directed professional (SDP), one who regularly sets and pursues ambitious personal and professional goals. Entropy is always tugging practitioners back toward the easy and familiar, the tried and true, the already prepared material that they know will work at some level of acceptability. The SDP, guided by a vision of a better way, regularly pushes forward toward better practices that promise more successful and long-lasting experiences for students and more rewarding experiences for himself or herself. The process outlined in the SDL learning proposal or contract serves as an excellent guide for personal and professional development too: creating a vision; setting a specific goal to pursue; planning the steps required to reach the desired goal; organizing the materials, people, and time required; setting the standards for success; and planning the celebration when that success is achieved.

Teaching is a celebratory activity. We work to make a significant difference in our students' lives. Students pursue their challenges in the field; the challenge teachers undertake is the program itself. When students celebrate their successes, teachers celebrate theirs as well—the self-directed learner guided by the self-directed professional.

Individual and *self-directed* do not mean "isolated" and "lonely" for students and should not for teachers either. The support group, the working journal, and the computer are as important to the SDP as they are to students of SDL. Teachers in motion should be affiliated with other teachers on the move. It is essential to find others who are winning, or want to be winning, in their professional lives. Seek them out. Find at least two to meet with regularly to share your plans, offer feedback, suggest ideas, give support, and provide help. Ideally, your support group members will also be learning SDL practices, but any professional development will do as long as everyone wants to grow. The support group meets regularly and provides the contact anyone who is moving in a new direction needs. Trying anything new arouses resistance of many kinds. The support group is an important bulwark against alienation. Things will go wrong. The support group is there to help solve the problems when they arise. These groups may continue for some time and result in lasting friendships. Helping each other does that.

The working journal becomes the teacher's silent companion and a record of his or her work as a self-directed professional. The computer is the teacher's means of connecting with both the vast resources for SDL and with other people who are involved in SDL or want to be. Teachers will find many schools involved in self-direction and can begin or join a network of other teachers who are teaching SDL. Teachers will also benefit by becoming politically skillful, which means becoming well connected to those who have influence on them and their programs. Teachers have a much greater chance for success when they have supportive contacts in the school administration, on the school board, and among parents. When questions arise in these arenas, there is then someone on hand who understands and can explain, and when issues arise, there is someone to speak on the teacher's behalf. Involving parents has the additional advantage of increasing their support and improving the performance of students.

When teachers choose to implement a program in SDL, they launch an experience with several payoffs. They offer a program for the future that empowers students for a life of learning. They launch a program of professional development that will equip them with a full repertoire of professional skills. Their pursuit of ambitious SDL projects is an inspiration and an influential model to their students. And they learn firsthand about the struggles and rewards involved in teaching self-direction.

Making a Difference to the Student

The individual teacher, or a team of teachers, can implement an SDL program in a TDL environment, but the two formats are not hospitable to each other, and success requires overcoming a number of obstacles. When the program is implemented in a school-within-a-school or a school is devoted to SDL, the individual teacher thrives. Fortunately, there are a number of convincing reasons that communities and school officials should now look favorably on establishing schools based on self-directed learning.

The paradigm of appropriate learning for adolescents has shifted from TDL to SDL. Research now points firmly to the enduring features of SDL as essential for success in learning, business, and life. A sedentary, abstract, anonymous factory approach to education is an inappropriate response to the demands of adolescent development: the cerebral, social, physical, and emotional changes that maturation presses on them; the crisis of character formation; and the transition to adulthood that lies immediately ahead. Like learning itself, growing demands aspiration, personal struggle, affiliation, and purposeful action. The means of meeting these demands are provided by SDL.

Large schools, especially large TDL schools, breed student isolation, anonymity, and alienation. Smaller schools, especially smaller SDL schools, foster involvement, identification, and affiliation. The focus in self-direction is on the individual, on teaching students to take control of their own learning, their own becoming, their own lives. When the prevailing spirit is affiliation, the consequences of alienation, graffiti, threats, destruction, and violence disappear or are greatly reduced. The large, traditional public TDL school is also facing a dislocation of purpose and the challenge of alternative choices for students that they are taking in ever greater numbers. In the decades immediately following World War II, schooling could safely predict that completing school and continuing through college would lead to a life of security and prosperity. In a world of rapid economic change and temporary contracted work, this promise can no longer be kept. In the meantime, home schooling, cyberschooling, private schooling, and specialized or magnet schooling are drawing students, often the best students, away from traditional schools. SDL provides teachers and administrators with an excellent response to these issues: the promise of a learning community in which teachers and administrators work together to prepare students to be skilled, knowledgeable, productive, self-reliant, cooperative, civil, and caring members of society. (Resource J lists some of the many ways in which students learn.)

Despite the difficulties it faces, schooling remains the one institution at the center of our hope for a thriving, civilized democratic society. Both kinds of schools may play a part. Traditional TDL schooling, especially schools where teachers do everything possible to infuse meaning and purpose into their teaching, meets the needs of many students. In any district, however, there are many students whom TDL schools do not serve well at all—students who urgently need an SDL school. As one superintendent said, "Our open school is essential to our district. There is a cohort of students—some of our brightest, some of our unnoticed, and some of our most difficult—who would be lost to us without it." SDL creates a place where all students can be successful and where most can achieve outstanding results. Every teacher and every element in the design of the program is focused on helping every student to find the desire, will, and determination to succeed and to succeed at levels they never before thought possible. Those outstanding achievements are another excellent reason for establishing SDL schools. Students do amazing things; a very high percentage of graduates go on to higher learning, where they have a high rate of success because they are clear in their goals and skilled at working independently to achieve their challenging visions. If the skills required for district and national tests are included in the list of required student outcomes, they will achieve those as well.

The most important reason for launching an SDL school, however, is that it is designed to serve students at the personal and social levels of experience as well as the intellectual level. An SDL school is a caring school, and every individual experiences that caring every day. Students are active participants in their classrooms, regularly consulted about their individual plans and challenges; they meet in triads, advisory groups, and seminars; they confer regularly with teachers. In many SDL schools, they also participate in school governance. In nearly all of these meetings, the topic is students' initiatives—anything that impedes them as well as everything that can be brought to bear to ensure that they will be accomplished successfully. Students do not pass unseen through SDL schools.

Starting an SDL School

An SDL school begins with a group of interested teachers who either find an opportunity themselves or respond to one provided by the district. Teachers may find one another through their own efforts to create an SDL classroom, in workshops and conferences, or on the Internet. District superintendents can create opportunities for new schools or schools-within-a-school to be developed. They can encourage teachers with support for individual SDL classroom initiatives and for teams of teachers to integrate their self-directed programs. The imperative for the teacher is to find others, at hand if possible or around the world on the Web if necessary. The imperative for the district leader taking the initiative is to provide opportunity, resources, support, and protection from the forces of conventionality over sufficient time to enable the school and its program to be designed, equipped, and rehearsed. The principal of the school is critical. That person must understand and be committed to the SDL concept and to the principle of collaborative decision making. He or she must also provide coherence by remaining through at least the first three to five years of the new program.

Preparing a school for opening is a challenging task, but it also offers many opportunities to create a supportive infrastructure. The healthy SDL school is under continual development; it is a learning school in which students learn from the environment, the management system, and the modeling of the faculty, as well as from the curriculum and what it offers. The teachers model SDL and its principles. The environment is open, emphasizing the discipline developing in students rather than external discipline—the regulations and consequences designed to enforce a code of visible order. Teachers emphasize connection, trust, affiliation, and caring relationships with students. This emphasis on connection extends throughout the students' school experience, which is designed to link them into networks of peers and adults through classes, groups, trips, apprenticeships, their passage activities, and school governance meetings.

These features, and the others we will discuss briefly, thrive best in a school of five hundred to eight hundred students, after which numbers generate anonymity, regulations, and alienation. Governance meetings held between staff and students to deal with school issues and activities highlight the emphasis in SDL schools on participation, democracy, and collaboration at all levels and in all activities. This process is a natural extension of the empowerment of students and the basic precept that students have both a right and a responsibility to speak and act on their behalf, on the behalf of others, and on behalf of the school. Democratic collaboration also characterizes the relationships among teachers and between teachers and the administration. The curriculum is planned collaboratively; the schedule is designed to facilitate the SDL program and kept flexible to accommodate special events and opportunities, such as trips and apprenticeships. When problems arise, the administration fends them off or solves them collaboratively. As one teacher said, "Around here we're always talking to each other: teachers to teachers, students to teachers, students to students, and all of us to the principal and the directors. It's like one year-long conversation about how we can do things better."

Administrative Support for SDL

A number of administrative features, introduced early, create many opportunities for SDL and signal to everyone that the theoretical talk is ready to be walked. The first feature is self-selection. The principal and teachers must know that the school will feature SDL and that they will be developing the program, the learning materials, and the environment. They must choose to be in the school or be willing participants in it. SDL is a challenge for teachers that requires new skills and a new attitude toward learning and toward students. Students will learn in a very new way, full of freedom and opportunity but requiring a great deal of responsibility and a great deal more work and risk than they will face in a regular school program.

An orientation meeting should be presented to interested students and then parents in the year prior to enrollment to announce the nature and promise of SDL and to dispel fears about it. This is a time for administration and faculty to sell the program and to enlist parents in support roles for the school as well as students to attend it.

The second feature is providing both teachers and students with the time and resources that they will need to make the difficult transition from TDL to SDL. Teachers need lead time to develop the teaching skills that SDL requires, produce such materials as the learning guides that students will follow, and organize the school so that such unique features as trips, apprenticeships, and out-of-school passages can be accommodated. A year's lead time to develop the school program is not excessive, and more time may be required if designing and preparing the building is included in the process. Once the program is operating, teachers need to provide the time and strategies that will enable students to make the dynamic transition from doing as they are told to deciding what to do and how to do it well for themselves. Even after this transitional program, teachers should have a plan to accommodate students who are still struggling with independence, collaboration, and generativity.

Administrators in collaboration with teachers can select from a variety of scheduling options to support the elements of the special program that they design. A school for SDL needs a program for SDL, and that program can thrive only when the schedule and operating procedure to support it are in place. The school program can be designed to facilitate SDL in a number of ways. Classes can be scheduled for four days each week, with the fifth day left open for individual work and team projects. In another model, mornings are devoted to classes and afternoons to independent activities. A small school-within-a-school can be launched offering SDL supplemented by any other courses that the host school offers. A course can be offered in SDL each year and possibly a second course for team SDL activities. The emphasis in these courses can be on students selecting and pursuing a program of excellence in a field of personal choice as counterpoint to the broader general program. While it is important for them to go out far, it is also important for them to go in deep, and while it is valuable for them to know something about a lot of things, it is essential for them to know as much as possible about one thing. When students are each following an individual plan every day and there are no classes as we know them—when students are working through learning guides, for example—the structure is completely different. Students supply their individual schedules, and teachers organize the support systems: seminars, labs, conferences, and testing facilities. In some schools, students take trips, apprenticeships, and fieldwork when these possibilities arise with the understanding that they will keep up their studies in the classes they will be missing.

The SDL school reaps many benefits when parents are involved early and often. If they are left on the outside and not kept well informed, they may become resistant to what they think is going on. If they do not know, they will assume, and their assumptions may not be kind. Keep parents informed through notices or on the Internet (over 90 percent of homes now have computers), meet with them regularly, invite them to the classroom, and involve them in passage conferences and student-run assessment presentations. Parents can be very helpful both at home and at school. When they are involved, their level of support increases, and their children's cooperation and productivity improve. Some schools have parents and others serve on advisory committees to support the SDL program. They advise on the curriculum, work with special students and student groups, solve problems, arrange apprenticeship sites, assist with travel, and raise funds for trips and special resources.

Creating a Shared Vision

Administrators of SDL schools suggest that those who are beginning establish a clear, shared vision, start small and proceed slowly, and prepare to stay the course. A school faculty, once chosen, may begin by selecting the form of SDL the school will employ, developing their shared vision into a mission statement, and deciding on the support structures and materials that will make their vision achievable. The four modes of SDL discussed in this book—independent thinking, self-managed learning, self-planned learning, and self-directed learning—provide a mix of SDL approaches, a sequence of them, or a balance between TDL and SDL.

That choice will be determined by the emerging vision of the faculty and administration, a shared picture of what exactly it is that they are attempting to achieve. Once the features of this vision are clear, they can be shaped into a statement of the mission that the school will be designed to achieve. Such a statement serves several purposes. It acts as a guide to development and to answering the question that will often be asked over time: "What do I [or we] do next?" It will be a reminder of the team's purpose when the going is rough and people want to return to the safe and familiar. The mission statement communicates the nature of the program to students, parents, and the community. Here is an example of such a statement, drawn up by the teachers and administrators at Thomas Haney High School:

> **Mission Statement for Thomas Haney Secondary School**
>
> Our mission is to have everyone seek challenge and experience success. We are working together to ensure that students of Thomas Haney High School become ...
>
> *High quality producers* who create products and services that consistently reflect high standards; take responsibility for results; use time management skills effectively.
>
> *Collaborative workers* who express ideas and needs; accept and value the ideas and needs of others; work closely with others in a changing environment; find creative options and look for consensus; act with integrity; work cooperatively in both competitive and non-competitive environments.
>
> *Global citizens* who interact positively with people of varied cultures; identify the environmental impact of decisions and promote the health of the world's environment; promote the welfare of all people in the world.
>
> *Socially responsible contributors* who participate in the political process; live in accordance with the just laws of society; process,

assimilate and synthesize information to determine actions; participate in life-long learning and contribute to improving the welfare of others.

Self-actualized individuals who value themselves as positive, worthwhile people; set and achieve personal and social goals; assess information to solve problems; take responsibility for their own emotional and physical well-being.

Communicative persons who can interact using a variety of communication processes and information sources.

Creative contributors who develop creative solutions and implement new ideas; experiment and take risks; participate in and influence change.

Above all, teachers and administrators must be ready to stay the course. When teachers decide to launch an SDL program, they set themselves a challenge as surely as students do when they design their passages. Challenge means reaching for a goal that will be difficult to achieve. On the journey to the accomplishment of such goals, problems will arise, problems that may demand significant modifications in the approaches being taken. These difficulties are predictable. They are the means by which an initiative is made workable and successful. For this reason, it is essential that teachers working together to implement SDL meet regularly to study the performance of their program. Ask the hard questions. Gather feedback and examine it fearlessly. When something is not working well, consider alternatives, develop a promising one, and move forward.

The great value of SDL is that it creates a framework within which a school can become a learning community. In it, all participants strive for what the early Greeks called *areté,* excellence as a person—excellence as a student, excellence as a teacher, excellence as an administrator, and excellence as a parent. Students strive to master the outcomes of the curriculum and achieve the ambitious goals they set for themselves. They struggle to find out who they are by discovering what they can do in a setting where every one of them can achieve success. Teachers work together to design a powerful program and employ a broad array of skills to guide and encourage their students' efforts and to ensure that each student is successful in finding and developing passionate pursuits. Often, students and teachers learn together in shared investigations and projects in the school and in locations far afield, assisted by parents and supported by the administration. Such a learning community is the vision of SDL and our hope for a promising future.

How Much SDL Are You Teaching Now?

YOU ARE ALMOST CERTAINLY teaching SDL now. See how far down the scale you can check off items to indicate how much you are already doing. These items provide a starting point and suggest opportunities to make students aware of the method as a point of departure for them too. Add any appropriate items, using the blank space at the end of the list. Itemize your existing SDL foundation.

☐ I assign tasks in class and assign homework.

☐ I connect my lessons with the personal experiences of my students.

☐ I give students the opportunity to express and develop their personal opinions and judgments.

☐ I teach students skills that they can use for the rest of their lives, such as critical thinking, arguing from evidence, remembering, problem solving, and visualizing.

☐ I give students choices in assignments and study activities.

☐ I allow some students to work through the text or assignment sheets or packages independently for some part of the course.

☐ My students regularly pursue course activities in cooperative groups.

☐ I assign individual projects for some part of the course that lead to personal products.

☐ I sometimes begin the class with a question or problem that students and I work out cooperatively.

☐ I teach students how to set goals, plan activities, and conduct their own learning projects.

☐ I involve my students in out-of-school activities such as field trips, apprenticeships, university courses, fieldwork, or volunteer service activities.

☐ My students conduct their own assessment conferences with parents.

☐ I am consciously and strategically teaching my students to be self-directed learners.

☐ I hold conferences with students about their individual studies, proposals, and individual activities.

☐ I am already actively pursuing a course designed to produce skilled self-directed learners.

From this beginning, decide where you wish to go. A student's situation is outlined by past experiences, a current situation, and anticipation of the future. You may find it helpful to identify the same framework of where you are now. What watershed experiences have you had with SDL as either a learner yourself or as a teacher that you can draw from? What current situation can you identify that would motivate you to make a change to SDL? And what vision of the future with your class can you formulate that would urge you forward?

How Self-Directing Are You?
A Self-Assessment Instrument

EVERYONE is self-directed, but each of us is self-directed to a different degree. Some of us are ready to scale Mount Everest; some of us have a tough time getting up for a walk to the corner store. We are all at different stages of readiness in the attitudes and skills necessary for self-direction, just as we are all at different stages of expertise in the fields of action we choose to pursue.

To some degree, therefore, everyone will be working on a program within this program. You will be developing the attitudes and skills that contribute to successful action, as well as conducting the action itself. The diagnostic instrument that follows is designed to help you determine how ready you are and which of the inner states and outer behaviors deserve most attention.

For each of the items below, check the extreme statement that comes the closest to describing your general attitude or behavior now. This is for your use only.

1. *Influence:* The course of my life is most powerfully influenced by the decisions:

   ☐ I make for myself.

   ☐ others make for me.

2. *Effectiveness:* If I tried to change myself, my life, my relationships, or my skills, I would:

   ☐ be able to do it.

   ☐ have great difficulty.

3. *Challenge:* In the course of my day-to-day activities, I regularly:

   ☐ try to learn something new.

   ☐ do what has to be done and what I'm sure I can do.

4. *Self-direction:* When I need to learn something new, I prefer to:

   ☐ learn it on my own.

   ☐ have someone teach it to me.

5. *Excellence:* When I am doing a task, I:

   ☐ try to do it as well as I can.

   ☐ do only what I have to do.

6. *Vision:* As far as the future goes, I:

   ☐ see good things happening.

   ☐ try not to think about it.

7. *Clarity:* My ideas about what to do are:

   ☐ what I think and decide.

   ☐ usually what others tell me or expect me to do.

8. *Goal setting:* In my day-to-day life, I regularly:

   ☐ set goals for myself to achieve.

   ☐ take things as they come.

9. *Confidence:* When I think about teaching myself, I think that I would:

   ☐ be able to do a good job.

   ☐ likely have a lot of problems.

10. *Planning:* When I've got a job to do, I:

    ☐ think of a good way to get it done well.

    ☐ find the easiest way to finish quickly.

11. *Learning style:* When I have to learn something, I prefer:

    ☐ to do it in my own way.

    ☐ to be told and shown how to do it.

12. *Initiative:* When it comes to activities, I:

    ☐ nearly always have some kind of project or activity under way.

    ☐ spend most of my time watching television or hanging out with friends.

13. *Determination:* As far as staying with a task until it's done, I:

    ☐ usually finish what I start.

    ☐ don't finish much unless someone makes me.

14. *Management:* When I launch a project, I:

    ☐ organize my time and the resources I'll need so I can approach the task efficiently.

    ☐ get started when I can and find what I need when the need arises.

15. *Getting support:* When I launch an activity of my own, I:

    ☐ find others to work with me or help me.

    ☐ work alone, without interference from others.

16. *Giving support:* When I'm working with others, I:

    ☐ give them all the help I can.

    ☐ do my job and let them do theirs.

17. *Openness:* When new ideas or activities are suggested to me, I:

    ☐ participate as fully as possible and help others as much as I can.

    ☐ keep quiet and try not to get too involved with the group.

18. *Evaluation:* When I'm involved in an activity, I know how well I'm doing because:

    ☐ I judge my own performance.

    ☐ others judge me and tell me.

19. *Reflection:* As far as my inner life goes:

    ☐ I often stop for periods of quiet and think about my life.

    ☐ I'm busy most of the time; it feels strange to sit around thinking about yourself.

20. *Celebration:* I often feel:

    ☐ really good about what I've done.

    ☐ disappointed that things didn't work out better.

21. *Renewal:* In the course of my life:

    ☐ I see a path ahead that I want to follow.

    ☐ things happen and I deal with them.

22. *Attribution:* In my opinion, people succeed at tasks because:

☐ they have a clear goal and work hard.

☐ they are lucky and were born with talent for the task.

23. *Esteem:* I feel that I am:

☐ a good person who will do something important in life.

☐ something of a loser who is not living up to expectations.

24. *Self-worth:* Other people:

☐ like me and enjoy being with me or working with me.

☐ would choose a lot of other people to be with or work with before they chose me.

25. *Support:* When I have a difficult task to do:

☐ my family and friends encourage me and offer help.

☐ I am pretty much on my own.

26. *Character:* When I find myself in any situation:

☐ I have a set of values to guide my attitudes and actions.

☐ I do whatever works and gives me an advantage.

27. *Process:* Faced with any task:

☐ I can devise a process for doing it well.

☐ I wait to be told how to do it.

28. *Self-efficacy:* When I begin a task:

☐ I am usually confident that I can do it.

☐ I doubt that I will be able to get it done.

29. *Self-motivation:* Faced with a tough task that I know is important:

☐ I can get myself started and keep myself going.

☐ I delay taking action and find other things to do.

30. *Self-evaluation:* When I'm working on a task or have just finished it:

☐ I can judge accurately how well I am doing or how well I have done.

☐ I can't tell how well I've done until I see my grades.

The Passage Process

Your Name: _____   Adviser: _____

Passage: _____   Consultant: _____

The Proposal

- ☐ Develop an IDEA (a dream). Consider your readiness in terms of past experiences, skills, motivation, resources, and personal strengths.
- ☐ Meet with your ADVISER and TRIAD to talk about the idea. <u>Take notes on responses and suggestions.</u>
- ☐ Meet with your chosen PASSAGE CONSULTANT. <u>Take notes during the meeting.</u> Ask for help with anything you don't understand.
- ☐ Write a ROUGH DRAFT, using the guidelines below, along with specific Passage guidelines.

How to Write a Passage Proposal

1. Describe your Passage in the opening paragraph. You could use the newspaper format of who, what, when, where, why, and how. Try to make your statements as clear as possible: write them as if someone who knew nothing about the school were reading your proposal.

2. Tell why your Passage is a challenge to you and what risks (physical, financial, social, and intellectual) you expect to experience.

Reprinted with permission of the Jefferson County Open High School, Lakewood, Colorado.

3. Describe your preparation for this Passage. Include your strengths, past experiences, and training you plan to pursue prior to beginning.

4. Describe the resources you have (personal strengths—motivation, knowledge, skills, abilities; people; books; materials; etc.) and the resources you will need and how you will obtain them.

5. What do you anticipate to be your greatest obstacles, and how do you hope to overcome them?

6. Identify possible peripheral learning.

7. Describe your first step in beginning this Passage, and list your steps in order toward completion. A time line with checkpoints may be helpful.

8. How will you document this Passage? How will you show changes in skills, attitudes, behaviors, and knowledge?

9. State how you will know when this Passage is complete and the proposed date of completion.

☐ Give the rough draft to your adviser, triad, and consultant and ask for FEEDBACK. This will need to be <u>at least two weeks prior</u> to the planned meeting.

☐ Make revisions and write a FINAL DRAFT of the proposal. This process usually occurs more than once. It often takes more than two weeks for the rewriting process.

☐ Select and ask people to be on your PASSAGE COMMITTEE. It needs to include the following people: adviser, Passage consultant, and triad members. You may also invite other students, parents, or community mentors as appropriate.

☐ Schedule a PASSAGE MEETING TIME. Inform all members of the committee of the time and place for the meeting.

☐ Give a copy of the final polished draft of the proposal to each member of your Passage committee <u>at least one week prior to the meeting time.</u>

☐ At the PASSAGE MEETING, seek approval and suggestions from the committee; take notes to use in making further revisions or in carrying out the Passage and writing the wrap-up summary.

The Passage

Your adviser, Passage consultant, triad, and members of your committee are available to help. If you need to change what you are doing, they need to be consulted.

Document everything you do—journal, notes, photos, receipts, letters, or other relevant records. Be sure to date and sign all important documents.

The Wrap-Up

☐ Schedule a demonstration or display.

☐ Organize the documentation.

☐ Write a ROUGH DRAFT of the Passage summary with the help of the guidelines below, along with specific Passage guidelines.

How to Write a Passage Wrap-Up

1. Describe your Passage as you proposed it. The description should be written clearly, with attention to main events and/or highlights, so a person unfamiliar with you and/or the school could understand this experience. Balance a need to summarize the experience with the equal need to keep the life in your writing about this Passage experience.

2. Tell what you accomplished and how you know you reached your goals.

3. Tell what obstacles, challenges, and risks (perceived and real) you expected to encounter in this Passage and how you dealt with them. Describe unexpected events, setbacks, and opportunities. Explain whether your expectations were realistic.

4. Describe turning points or highlights within the experience. These can be documented with excerpts from your journal.

5. Describe peripheral or unanticipated learning that occurred in this Passage.

6. List all the resources used for this Passage. Be specific.

7. The closing statement could include the following: how you feel about yourself and the completion of this Passage, why this Passage has made a difference in your life, and where you will go from here in further exploration or experiences.

- ☐ Refer to specific Passage guidelines for additional information required for each wrap-up.
- ☐ Meet with your adviser for feedback and help.
- ☐ Meet with your triad for feedback and help.
- ☐ Meet with your Passage consultant for feedback and help. This may need to occur more than once.
- ☐ Submit your rough draft of the wrap-up at least two weeks before you intend to have your wrap-up meeting. Be sure to include a summary of things that you learned that were peripheral to the Passage or unexpected.
- ☐ Revise and write the FINAL DRAFT of the wrap-up, based on notes, suggestions, and feedback.
- ☐ Schedule a WRAP-UP MEETING TIME on a Walkabout Day. Inform all members of the committee of the time and place for the meeting.
- ☐ Give a copy of the final polished draft of the wrap-up to each member of your Passage committee <u>at least one week prior to the meeting time.</u>
- ☐ Present your accomplishments to your committee and CELEBRATE YOUR SUCCESS!

The Integrated SDL Unit
The Kinds of Activities Involved

	Experience	Study	Productive Activity
Personal—Individual	*Sensing-Feeling* Expanding direct experiences of reality. Increasing range and depth of perception. Seeking new experiences; discovering interests; becoming absorbed. Becoming self-aware; understanding feelings; developing imagination.	*Thinking* Accumulating knowledge about the world. Developing thinking skills; asking questions; gathering data; formulating concepts. Making decisions, plans. Reflecting on oneself and one's character and values.	*Acting* Extending one's ability to function in the world. Initiating activities; challenging oneself to act, seek adventure, launch inquiries, construct something practical, help others, create something imaginative, learn a job. Develop the skills of doing.
Interpersonal—Social	*Connection* Forming relationships with others. Meeting people; learning warmth, trust, and empathy; experiencing other lifestyles, races, and cultures; sharing, caring, and helping; experiencing new roles and social situations.	*Cooperation* Learning with others and from them. Learning to function in a group, to participate and to lead, to give and to receive feedback, to intervene and to solve problems. Sharing study activities; teaching others and learning from them.	*Teamwork* Accomplishing productive tasks with others. Learning to work together to achieve shared goals. Launching investigations, enterprises, contributions; taking group action on issues; traveling with others for a purpose. Developing group synergy.

	Experience	**Study**	**Productive Activity**
Impersonal— Academic-Technical	*Exploration* Seeking concrete experiences in fields of study. Attending and giving performances. Learning to use resources: museums, libraries, galleries, colleges, archaeological sites. Experiencing adventurous activities and work. Becoming curious, passionate, dedicated.	*Investigation* Pursuing formal studies of knowledge. Taking courses in school, on-line, through learning guides, or at college. Designing one's own formal studies to achieve course outcomes or one's own goals. Developing and pursuing personal questions and answers.	*Production* Undertaking projects to apply and to generate knowledge. Testing ideas; formulating opinions and arguments. Applying, experimenting, exploring, creating, building. Working at jobs. Initiating, persevering, accomplishing.

Inner States for SDL

ACTS THAT WE INITIATE are more often successful when our thoughts and feelings are in harmony with our intended statements and actions rather than in conflict with them.

Our intentional selves are in harmony with our intended acts when we

- Decide on goals with clarity.

- Plan with confidence.

- Manage ourselves and our actions with determination.

- Evaluate our success with openness.

- Seek renewal in reflection.

Inner State	Influence on Outer Action
Clarity: In the broadest sense, that you know what you value, who you are, and what you hope to do; in the specific sense, that you know the most appropriate thing for you to be doing now	A clear statement of a goal of great personal importance
Confidence: In the broadest sense, your feeling that you can plan, you can act, and you will be successful; in the specific sense, that you can risk a significant challenge and strategically achieve it	A challenging, workable plan that ensures the achievement of the goal

The Self-Directed Learning Handbook by Maurice Gibbons.

Inner State	Influence on Outer Action
Determination: In the broadest sense, that you have self-control and can keep at the task until it is complete; in the specific sense, that you can successfully complete a single task you set for yourself	A personalized management procedure that supplies what is needed for enacting the plan and ensures its completion.
Openness: In the broadest sense, that you are open to ideas, information about yourself, and change; in the specific sense, that you will openly seek and consider information about the quality of your performance in the task ahead	A realistic procedure for monitoring progress and judging the quality of the results of your efforts
Reflection: In the broadest sense, that you think about the meaning and significance of life issues; in the specific sense, that you think about what you have learned from your self-directed action and what you will pursue next	A thoughtful review of the experience and projection into possible future improvements and achievements—renewal

When our thoughts and feelings are out of harmony with our intended statements and actions, we undermine our efforts and diminish our potential for success.

Productive Inner Responses	Unproductive Inner Responses
Clarity: "I know that I want to accomplish and become."	*Confusion:* "I've never really thought about it. I have no idea what to do."
Confidence: "I am worthwhile; I can act. I will be successful."	*Helplessness:* "I can't change things. I'm not very good at this. I'll likely fail."
Determination: "I have the energy and will to do this for myself. I will finish, and my results will be good."	*Doubt:* "Something will go wrong. Something always does. I never seem to finish what I start."

Productive Inner Responses

Openness: "I want to know how well I'm doing so I can learn from success and failure."

Reflection: "I spend some quiet time making sense of what I've done and thinking about the possibilities of the future."

Unproductive Inner Responses

Closedness: "Who knows if I've done well or not? If I haven't, I'd rather not know or let anyone else find out."

Distraction: "I'm too busy to sit around, and when I have time, I entertain myself. Besides, when it's done, it's done."

Resource F

Sample Process Templates

PROCESS TEMPLATES are skills organized into procedures—patterns of activity—for getting tasks of a certain kind done well. Each template can be applied to any activity of its kind. Be prepared to modify the procedure when the situation requires it.

Action Template

Informed action is the engine that all learning fuels.

Analyze critical issues.

Study the issue from all sides.

Plan a course of action.

Organize for action.

Take action.

Choose a significant issue.

Select and develop a point of view.

Rehearse performance skills.

Gather resources, prepare.

Evaluate and modify action.

Examples: Taking action to preserve the environment; taking action in the political process; taking action to help someone in need or trouble or to correct a wrong; acting to resolve social problems.

Competence Template

Becoming good at something useful is the bridge between our dreams and reality.

Analyze your interests, talents.

Survey the field.

Observe specialists in the field.

Plan a program of study and practice.

Set a challenge in your field.

Review the process and achievement.

Choose a field of specialty.

Confirm, commit to chosen specialty.

List knowledge, skills needed.

Enact plan in key field area.

Plan and execute challenge.

Reconfirm, pursue specialty.

Examples: Becoming competent in a field of work; becoming competent in a vocational or recreational field; improving competence in any field.

Teamwork Template

When we merge our intent with others', we multiply our energy and impact and become briefly tribal.

Select a diverse group.

Get to know each other.

Share concerns and interests.

Develop operating procedure.

Identify individual roles.

Review task and group success.

Meet as a group.

Build member relationships.

Choose an issue, goal, or purpose.

Plan how to achieve goal.

Execute your plan.

Renew, celebrate, close.

Examples: Taking part in any team or group with a task; heading any team; setting up any team. Teams play sports, run organizations, have specific tasks to accomplish or problems to solve, run campaigns, and so on.

Expression Template

Expressing our truth shapes us, defines our character, and makes the best of us accessible to others.

Select issue or idea to be expressed.

Consider situation and audience.

Examine models of excellence.

Generate outlines, sketches, models.

Compose initial expression.

Present for informed feedback.

Clarify your point of view.

Determine medium and impact.

Visualize desired outcome.

Rehearse skills; practice.

Examine critically; repeat if needed.

Complete final expression for presentation.

Examples: Formulating and expressing an opinion or position; creating a film, story, painting, or other creative work.

Guidelines, Traps, and Boosters

Guidelines

Only You Can Make Yourself Powerful

These activities are all designed to help you become powerful. Power is simply the ability to make things happen: to learn, to act, to change, to build, to make a difference. But the system in these activities is an empty shell without your dreams, energy, and drive. Some people choose to be helpless. We urge you to seek your power. Only you can do it.

Learn Something Every Day That You Can Use for the Rest of Your Life

The skills and procedures in these activities can be used to learn and do anything for the rest of your life. Recognize important knowledge, skills, and processes, and learn them. Use what you learn in other parts of your life.

Know Something About Everything and Everything About Something

A good general knowledge about the world is useful, but so is knowing a lot about something in particular and being good at it. Find a field that really interests you, and work hard to become very good at it. Become an expert.

Think!

Don't just follow the crowd or wait for instructions. Think for yourself. All of us can; few of us do. Talk to yourself in your mind. Raise questions and find answers. Select important goals and make solid plans. Think about the person you want to be. Dream, and make your dreams come true.

The Only Real Failure Is an Event from Which You Learn Nothing

Many people are unsuccessful many times in their lives before they begin to achieve their highest goals. It is their way of learning how to get it right. In fact, the Wright brothers were unsuccessful with many designs before their airplane finally flew. Be courageous. Do not fear failure. Take the risk. Learn from difficulties. Move forward.

Be Proud!

Be someone worthy. Be proud you are not helpless, that you can teach yourself, that you can get things done. Cooperate with others; help them, and accept help from them. Pursue valuable goals. Celebrate achieving them.

Traps to Watch Out For

The Dreaded Deadly Plunge

Some people start with enthusiasm but fade when the responsibility and hard work hits them, or when they start running into problems.

If it happens to you, be realistic and determined. Pulling out of the plunge will be your most important challenge. Take a step at a time. Set achievable goals. Build a pattern of successes. Seek help. But get there.

The Long, Desperate Wait

Some people are so used to being told what to do that they feel lost when they have to decide for themselves. If they are good at schoolwork, they may get angry at a change in the way the work is presented, as with personal projects.

But if you think about it, a long, desperate wait for instructions isn't much fun. Managing personal projects is the other side of the learning coin. You need to develop skill in teaching yourself just as you did in learning from a teacher. Use the same skills that made you successful before. Think of the work in these activities as assignments if you need to. If you do them thoroughly, you will soon be taking charge.

The Search for Someone to Please

Some people choose projects they think others want them to choose. Then they lose interest in their work because their real interests lie somewhere else. The voices of others have so much power they can't hear their own.

If you take the time to sit quietly, you will hear your other voice talking to you. Think of the things you have done. Think about activities that felt good and made you proud. Remember your dreams. Let your inner voice speak; then act.

That Empty, Helpless Feeling

Some people make things happen; others wait for things to happen to them. They can't seem to get started, and, once finally started, they find it hard to keep going. Decisions terrify them.

You can decide and act. First, say, "Yes, making decisions is my problem." Recognize it, and you are on your way. List other options. Choose one, and get started. You can change the activity later if you need to, but get started now.

The Greasy Slide to Failure

Failure, like hell, is an unpleasant experience. Yet some people seem to do everything they can to be unsuccessful. You can watch them defeat themselves.

Remember that with each project, you start fresh. You can choose your project, and you can choose success. Silence the voices that say you are no good with your hands, not very bright, or afraid to try. Find your talent, and follow the path that excites you. Success is progress from where you are now. You can do that. We all can get better and better and better.

Boosters

The path to a successful project is seldom a smooth one. When you meet difficulties, problems, even disasters, much will depend on your attitude. People who are positive, confident, and determined usually prevail. So work on yourself to develop a "Yes, I can" attitude. Here are a few ways to boost yourself into drive.

Use Positive Self-Talk

When you talk to yourself in your mind, talk about yourself in a positive language. Say, "Yes, I can," "Yes, I will," and then, "Yes, I did." And check out any voices that say you can't or won't. Use your positive language to talk those voices down.

Build a Pattern of Success

Anything you accomplish that you haven't before is a success. Begin your project with steps you are confident that you can achieve. Then increase the level of challenge until you are reaching for your best performance. Success breeds success.

Keep a Wonderful Vision Before You

Fortunate people seldom actually achieve their visions, but a picture of the best results that they can imagine often leads them to progress they never thought possible. Form a picture of the best project you can imagine and of the life you want and the kind of person you want to be. Hold that vision in your mind as a guide and lure.

Act as If . . .

Sometimes we have to try on new attitudes and ways of doing things before they feel right. If you find it hard to be positive, confident, and determined, then act as if you are. Pretend. Try on the new behavior in safe circumstances until it fits comfortably.

Help Others

Helping others nearly always makes us feel good about ourselves. Find ways to be thoughtful and giving to family, friends, and others. Listen to them, support them, and help them. Give what you would most like to receive. It is what good friends and members of families and communities do. They contribute.

Resource H

The Support Group
or Triad

THERE WILL BE many different group organizations in your SDL program. Help students to build support groups of about three members each. These groups, or triads, meet regularly to discuss intentions, plans, and problems. They offer ideas and assistance, and they act as a preliminary preparation for advisory group meetings and individual conferences with their teacher. Support groups can be an important lifeline for students, and they provide an important training ground for the development of interpersonal attitudes and skills. Most human interaction involves cooperation. Working well with others may be the most important lifelong skill that students can learn. Here are a few important skills and attitudes about working with others that students in support groups need to know.

Group work is cooperative. Students must learn what Johnson and Johnson (1991) call positive interdependence, that state in which all group members see a common goal, realize that it can be achieved only by working together, and determine to shape their behavior and effort for the common good. In the beginning, foster a group feeling by clearly stating the responsibilities each student has to the other members of the group, and then make it clear that they will also enjoy many benefits.

Build group feeling by creating experiences the three students can enjoy together, such as a shared lunch or a visit to a museum or other interesting place. Give them tasks to complete together, such as visiting and helping out at a children's hospital or a home for the elderly. Set problems to solve, study assignments, or other learning tasks that the triad can complete cooperatively.

The support group is a team with a job to do: to make sure that each group member completes his or her SDL tasks successfully. Students need to know what that involves and how to accomplish it. The basic responsibilities are to meet regularly, review each member's proposals and progress, offer suggestions, and offer help when other group members need it. Students often come to the group with problems. To help, all members should be skilled at problem solving: specifying the problem, generating solutions, and choosing one solution to develop.

The next step is to teach students how to function efficiently as a support group. This means following such procedures as setting an agenda, sharing conversation time equally, and dealing with problems that the members have in working together. The best way to introduce these skills and attitudes is through role playing.

One key to group success is everyone's willingness to contribute their best and hold back their worst. Every member at any moment is building or draining group energy. Learning to build by contributing ideas, resources, encouragement, and energy is critical. Learning to attend to others and to respond to them when they speak also builds the group. Distracting behavior, corrosive comments, and constant criticism drain its energy. One way to introduce this theme is to collect ideas from students to list what kinds of behavior drains group energy and what kinds build it. Make a chart of these behaviors, and keep it in view.

In the same way a car runs on gas, groups run on communication. Communication, first of all, means that everyone makes sure that they hear from everyone else in their group. Second, it means paying attention to what everyone else says, making sure they all understand and asking questions until they do. Third, it means responding and contributing thoughtfully and clearly. Use practice activities to help students learn these skills.

The group needs to establish early that it is a safe place to be, a safe place to take part, and a safe place to be authentic. The members have to trust each other not to humiliate anyone who is self-revealing, not to severely criticize suggestions made by others, and not to violate anyone's privacy by talking outside the group. A questionnaire about what trust is, how one exhibits it, and how one violates it can focus on key issues for a group and a class discussion.

Teach students to enter discussions with a negotiator's attitude: "I can't demand that everyone else agree with me, and I won't necessarily agree with everyone else's position, but I will cooperate fully in building a decision that we can all agree with. So let's hear from everyone, and then create consensus around the most central ideas." Hearing from everyone, being willing to yield, contributing to an agreed-on decision or plan, and becoming committed to it are challenging tasks. Describe the challenge, and then assign decision making. This is the principle of negotiation, of "getting to yes"—that new position that everyone can agree with.

Groups can have a strong leader, or all of the members can be leaders. Participation creates ownership and commitment; silence and passivity create indifference. Anyone can say, "Let's get started" or "What's the first order of business?" or "Let's draw up an agenda." A group that operates by shared leadership can also call for a leader to chair the group when the situation demands speed and efficiency.

When groups hit the doldrums or reach a crisis, it is time for group processing: stepping away from the task, standing back, and reviewing exactly how the group reached the impasse, explosion, or malaise that made it dysfunctional. Teach students to observe as if from a distance and as if they are strangers. Encourage them to be fair witnesses to what happened: focus on resolving the problem, not self-interest. Show the group how to generate alternatives, select a better pattern of operation, and put it into practice. Use a process observer to watch and take notes and then give the group feedback about the way it is operating.

Because group work is an important element of any SDL program, it is essential to help students to become skillful in these participation skills. The work of the support groups is very valuable to students and to teachers of SDL. With the help of their groups, students learn to solve many of their own problems, and they present more workable proposals. They learn how to be a part of the social world around them, and they learn about themselves as members of it.

Samples from a Student's Working Journal

THE FOLLOWING SAMPLES illustrate the kinds of entries that are included in a working journal: quotations, research, observations, ideas, plans, reports, and reflections.

The harder I work, the luckier I seem to get.

—MARK TWAIN

Myth is depersonalized dream; dream is personalized myth.

—JOSEPH CAMPBELL, *Hero with a Thousand Faces*

Two Mosquitoes flew at zero feet to the Clermont-Cognac areas. There they sighted a loaded munitions train heading north and made three passes with cannon and machine guns. On the third pass, one car exploded, igniting several others and sending debris up all around the attackers. Four FW 109s attacked as they broke away to starboard from their final pass. The section, low on ammunition, took cloud cover and returned to base.

—Combat report of Flight Lieutenant James Noel Tanner, March 1943

De Havilland Mosquito Mk NF V1. A World War II fighter-bomber manufactured secretly by De Havilland from smooth-stress plywood sheeting and first commissioned in May 1943, the

Mosquito was powered by twin Merlin 1250 hp engines with a range of 1500 miles, a cruising speed between 255 and 300 mph and a maximum speed of 436 mph. Armed with four 20mm cannon and four .303 caliber machine guns, and capable of carrying four 500 lb. bombs, the Mosquito conducted day ranger attacks on enemy airfields, became a night-intruder on special missions and attacked buzz-bombs aimed for London.

—*Fighter Planes of World War II*

September 12

I am fascinated by my grandfather's experience as a Mosquito pilot in the Second World War. He was a hero, I think, but he won't talk about it. I can't imagine what it is like to face death every day. I can't even imagine what it is like to fly a small plane, without even being in combat.

I have to start somewhere. This may be the best place. I'd like to know more about the Mosquito, the war and about flying. The best place to start is another talk with granddad.

September 15

I am fascinated by war. I am also against it. Whether it is Korea, Vietnam, South Africa or the Middle East, it always seems to be the rich and powerful attacking the poor and less developed. Even in our own armies, it is the poor, less educated minorities who end up fighting and dying. And although we give high blown reasons, we usually go to war so we can keep our riches and power. The pain such wars cause, mostly to civilians, is horrible. So here I am fascinated by war but opposing it too.

September 19

My real interest is in flying. I want to solo before I leave high school. There is one small problem though. It costs a fortune and I don't even have a job. So here is my list of possibilities:

- Research the story of my granddad's flying career.
- Make a visual history of the air war in WWII.
- Build a flying model of the Mosquito.
- Learn to fly and solo.
- Work for an anti-war group.
- Plan my own peace campaign.

All of these things interest me. That's a surprise. I always say I don't have any interests. It makes hanging out easier. My first choice is building an airplane model. Dad and I used to make gliders when I was younger. Aunt Maude is going to give me some space and some help, too. I know I can get granddad involved in this one.

September 22

Goal: To build and fly a gas-driven, remote-controlled model of a Mosquito fighter-bomber. This includes Goal #2, raising the money to do Goal #1.

Plan:

- Track down and buy a kit for the Mosquito.
- Build the model.
- Fly the model. (How do I learn to use remote or hand controls without putting my model in danger?)
- Practice take-offs, landings, and maneuvers.

Challenge: Look up meets and competitions. Enter one.

September 29

My first problem; there is no kit for the Mosquito. I decided to make the kit myself. It's a big move but I've found a model-making club at school. Some people make their stuff from scratch and will show me how, but it will take a lot longer. Everything else is going okay. My aunt and granddad are on board and I've even got a lead on a motor I can borrow or trade for. I want to fly it now. I'm not good at waiting.

October 6

There are three things I'm having trouble with: doing what I say I'm going to do, doing the hard work that leads up to the good stuff, and this reflecting. Thinking about myself feels funny, like I shouldn't be doing it. Maybe I'm scared a bit, too. If you look at what you are doing, if you think about it, you can't deny it any more. You have to explain it, maybe justify it. And what if you looked at what you are doing and you didn't like it? Or you looked inside and didn't see anything? It scares me. Is that what this is all about?

When I should be working on the model, I want to be finished and to be flying it. I avoid getting to work and when I do get to work I get frustrated that it's taking so long and that I can't finish that day. So I've looked at that. Now what? What good did that do?

October 9

Like Dad says, "Take life as it comes." I have my doubts about this thinking everything through, about trying to figure out the meaning of life. I want to fly and there isn't much more to say than that.

December 5

Wonders never cease. As Mrs. Gordon says, "When you take initiative, all kinds of things start to happen." At a model airplane meet I met Carl Mancowitz in a wheelchair who can't fly anymore. He still has his plane and offered me to use it for lessons if I can find someone qualified to teach me. When I told Grandpa, he said he would put up half the money for lessons if I raise the rest. He wants me to work. I know it. I know I want to fly so I can make my career challenge to get a job and earn my half. I'll do flying as my practical challenge with a solo as my demo. And why not do my logical inquiry as navigation? Mrs. Gordon found a friend of a friend who is taking me up next Sunday. I can't wait. First time!

Some of the Many Ways Students Can Learn

- Learn by being told—through lessons, lectures, presentations.
- Learn by being shown—from examples, demonstrations, and models.
- Learn from an on-line or distance education course.
- Learn by observing intensely.
- Learn by studying books or other print resources.
- Learn by asking someone what you want to know.
- Learn by searching the Internet.
- Learn by imitating a skilled performance.
- Learn by practicing repeatedly, especially coached practice.
- Learn by mentally rehearsing.
- Learn by seeking direct experiences.
- Learn by conducting an experiment.
- Learn by taking action in the field, by doing it.
- Learn by working cooperatively with others as a team.
- Learn by teaching someone else.
- Learn by teaching yourself.
- Learn by studying media: videos, CDs, tapes, and DVDs.
- Learn by preparing a public presentation.
- Learn by working or studying with a mentor.
- Learn by trial and error.
- Learn by dramatization, by acting it out.

- Learn by grouping, categorizing, and clarifying.
- Learn by forming concepts based on evidence and reason.
- Learn by creating conceptual maps of relationships among items or ideas.
- Learn by picturing—by seeing and recalling things that are.
- Learn by visualizing—by imagining things that might be.
- Learn by thinking metaphorically: link the known to the unknown.
- Learn about ideas by connecting them to what you already know.
- Learn from failure how not to fail; from success, how to succeed.
- Learn from simulations.
- Learn by taking a job that requires the performance you seek.
- Learn by thinking for yourself—forming opinions, reaching conclusions.
- Learn intuitively: discover what you know instinctively.
- Learn by competing with others.
- Learn by playing spontaneously or in games.
- Learn from observing yourself: your thoughts, emotions, and actions.
- Learn by striving to achieve an ambitious goal.
- Learn from reflection and contemplation in solitude.
- Learn from travel—new places, new people, new activities.
- Learn by doing what has moral value (for example, helping others).
- Learn by seeking feedback from others about your performance.
- Learn by keeping a working journal of ideas, plans, and reflections.
- Learn from a model of outstanding performance.
- Learn by developing effective processes for getting things done.
- Learn by challenging yourself to reach a new level of performance.

Bibliography

Bandura, A. *Social Learning Theory.* Upper Saddle River, N.J.: Prentice-Hall, 1977.

Becker, E. *The Birth and Death of Meaning.* New York: Free Press, 1971.

Bligh, D. A. *What's The Use of Lectures?* San Francisco: Jossey-Bass, 2000.

Blythe, T., and Associates. *The Teaching for Understanding Guide.* San Francisco: Jossey-Bass, 1998.

Bransford, J. D., Brown, A. L., and Cocking, R. R. (eds.). *How People Learn: Brain, Mind, Experience, and School.* Washington, D.C.: National Academy Press, 1999.

Brown, J. L., and Moffett, C. A. *The Hero's Journey: How Educators Can Transform Schools and Improve Learning.* Alexandria, Va.: Association for Supervision and Curriculum Development, 1999.

Brownlie, F., Close, S., and Walgren, L. *Tomorrow's Classroom Today: Strategies for Creating Active Readers, Writers and Thinkers.* Markham, Ontario: Pembroke Publishers, 1990.

Bruning, R. H., Schraw, G. J., and Ronning, R. R. *Cognitive Psychology and Instruction.* Upper Saddle River, N.J.: Prentice Hall, 1995.

Buckingham, M., and Clifton, D. O. *Now, Discover Your Strengths.* New York: Free Press, 2001.

Campbell, J. *The Power of Myth.* New York: Doubleday, 1988.

Candy, P. C. *Self-Direction for Lifelong Learning: A Comprehensive Guide to Theory and Practice.* San Francisco: Jossey-Bass, 1991.

Costa, A. L., and Liebmann, R. M. (eds.). *Envisioning Process as Content: Toward a Renaissance Curriculum.* Thousand Oaks, Calif.: Corwin Press, 1997.

Covey, S. R. *The Seven Habits of Highly Effective People: Restoring the Character Ethic.* New York: Simon & Schuster, 1989.

Csikszentmihalyi, M. *Flow: The Psychology of Optimal Experience.* New York: HarperCollins, 1990.

Csikszentmihalyi, M. *Creativity: Flow and the Psychology of Discovery and Invention.* New York: HarperCollins, 1996.

Della-Dora, D., and Blanchard, L. J. (eds.). *Moving Toward Self-Directed Learning.* Alexandria, Va.: Association for Supervision and Curriculum Development, 1979.

Dunn, K. J., and Dunn, R. S. *Teaching Secondary School Students Through Their Individual Learning Styles.* Needham Heights, Mass.: Allyn and Bacon, 1993.

Erikson, E. H. *Identity and the Life Cycle.* New York: International Universities Press, 1959.

Flavell, J. H. *Cognitive Development.* Upper Saddle River, N.J.: Prentice Hall, 1977.

Fobes, R. *The Creative Problem Solver's Toolbox.* Corvallis, Ore.: Solutions Through Innovation, 1993.

Ford, M. E. *Motivating Humans: Goals, Emotions and Personal Agency Beliefs.* Thousand Oaks, Calif.: Sage, 1992.

Fullan, M. *The New Meaning of Educational Change.* New York: Teachers College Press, 1991.

Gardner, H. *The Disciplined Mind.* New York: Penguin Books, 1999.

Gibbons, M. *Individualized Instruction: A Descriptive Analysis.* New York: Teachers College Press, 1971.

Gibbons, M. "Walkabout: Searching for the Right Passage from Childhood and School." *Phi Delta Kappan,* May 1974, pp. 596–602.

Gibbons, M. *The New Secondary Education: A Phi Delta Task Force Report.* Bloomington, Ind.: Phi Delta Kappa, 1976.

Gibbons, M. *The Walkabout Papers: Challenging Students to Challenge Themselves.* Vancouver, Canada: EduServ, 1990.

Gibbons, M. *How to Become an Expert.* Tucson, Ariz.: Zephyr Press, 1991.

Gilmore, J. V. *The Productive Personality.* San Francisco: Albion Publishing, 1974.

Gladwell, M. *The Tipping Point: How Little Things Can Make a Big Difference.* New York: Little, Brown, 2000.

Goleman, D. *Working with Emotional Intelligence.* New York: Bantam Books, 1998.

Gross, R. *Peak Learning: A Master Course in Learning How to Learn.* Los Angeles: Jeremy P. Tarcher, 1991.

Hacker, D., Dunlosky, J., and Graesser, A. *Metacognition in Educational Theory and Practice.* Mahwah, N.J.: Erlbaum, 1998.

Hargreaves, A. (ed.). *Rethinking Educational Change with Heart and Mind: 1997 ASCD Yearbook.* Alexandria, Va.: Association for Supervision and Curriculum Development, 1997.

Hargreaves, A., and Fullan, M. *What's Worth Fighting For out There?* Mississauga, Ontario: Ontario Public School Teachers' Federation, 1998.

Hester, J. P. *Teaching for Thinking.* Durham, N.C.: Carolina Academic Press, 1994.

Holt, J. *How Children Fail.* New York: Dell, 1964.

Hyerle, D. *Visual Tools for Constructing Knowledge.* Alexandria, Va.: Association for Supervision and Curriculum Development, 1996.

Johnson, D. W., and Johnson, R. T. *Learning Together and Alone: Cooperative, Competitive, and Individualistic Learning.* Needham Heights, Mass.: Allyn and Bacon, 1991.

Kelly, G. A. *The Psychology of Personal Constructs.* New York: Norton, 1955.

Kohn, A. *No Contest: The Case Against Competition.* Boston: Houghton Mifflin, 1992.

Kolb, D. A. *Experiential Learning: Experience as the Source of Learning and Development.* Upper Saddle River, N.J.: Prentice Hall, 1984.

Martorella, Peter H. *Concept Learning: Designs for Instruction.* Scranton, Pa.: Intext Educational Publishers, 1972.

Maslow, A. H. *The Farther Reaches of Human Nature.* New York: Viking Press, 1971.

Neill, A. S. *Summerhill: A Radical Approach to Child Rearing.* New York: Hart Publishing, 1964.

Neve, C. D., Hart, L. A., and Thomas, E. C. "Huge Learning Jumps Show Potency of Brain-Based Instruction." *Phi Delta Kappan,* Oct. 1988, pp. 143–148.

Oram, A., Minac, N., and Shirky, C. *Peer-to-Peer: Harnessing the Power of Disruptive Technologies.* Cambridge, Mass.: O'Reilly & Associates, 2001.

Oshry, B. *Seeing Systems: Unlocking the Mysteries of Organizational Life.* San Francisco: Berrett-Koehler, 1996.

O'Sullivan, E. *Transformative Learning: Educational Vision for the Twenty-First Century.* London: Zed Books, 1999.

Piskurich, G. M. *Self-Directed Learning: A Practical Guide to Design, Development, and Implementation.* San Francisco: Jossey-Bass, 1993.

Polanyi, M. *Personal Knowledge: Towards a Post-Critical Philosophy.* Chicago: University of Chicago Press, 1974.

Reisman, D. *The Lonely Crowd.* New Haven, Conn.: Yale University Press, 1950.

Riding, R. *Cognitive Styles and Learning Strategies: Understanding Style Differences in Learning and Behaviour.* London: Taylor and Francis, 1998.

Robinson Masters, N. *Fighter Planes of World War II*. Mankato, Minn.: Capstone High/Low, 1999.

Rogers, C. *Freedom to Learn for the '80s*. Columbus, Ohio: Charles E. Merrill, 1983.

Samples, B. *Openmind/Wholemind: Parenting and Teaching Tomorrow's Children Today*. Rolling Hills Estates, Calif.: Jalmar Press, 1987.

Seligman, M.E.P. *Learned Optimism*. New York: Knopf, 1990.

Seligman, M.E.P. *The Optimistic Child*. Boston: Houghton Mifflin, 1995.

Senge, P. M. *The Fifth Discipline: The Art and Practice of the Learning Organization*. New York: Doubleday, 1990.

Senge, P. M. (ed.). *Schools That Learn: A Fifth Discipline Fieldbook for Educators, Parents and Everyone Who Cares About Education*. New York: Doubleday, 2000.

Senge, P. M., and Associates. *The Fifth Discipline Fieldbook*. New York: Doubleday, 1994.

Sheehy, G. *New Passages: Mapping Your Life Across Time*. New York: Ballantine Books, 1995.

Sizer, T. *Horace's School: Redesigning the American High School*. Boston: Houghton Mifflin, 1992.

Smiles, S. *Self-Help; with Illustrations of Conduct and Perseverance*. London: John Murray, 1884.

Smith, F. *Insult to Intelligence: The Bureaucratic Invasion of our Classrooms*. New York: Arbor House, 1986.

Smith, R. M. (ed.). *Theory Building for Learning How to Learn*. Chicago: Educational Studies Press, 1987.

Smith, R. M., and Associates. *Learning to Learn Across the Life Span*. San Francisco: Jossey-Bass, 1990.

Sprenger, M. *Learning and Memory: The Brain in Action*. Alexandria, Va.: Association for Supervision and Curriculum Development, 1999.

Sternberg, R. J. *Successful Intelligence: How Practical and Creative Intelligence Determine Success in Life*. New York: Plume, 1997.

Tileston, D. W. *Ten Best Teaching Practices: How Brain Research, Learning Styles and Standards Define Teaching Competencies*. Thousand Oaks, Calif.: Corwin Press, 2000.

Trump, J. L. *A School for Everyone*. Reston, Va.: National Association of Secondary School Principals, 1977.

Vaill, P. B. *Learning as a Way of Being: Strategies for Survival in a World of Permanent White Water*. San Francisco: Jossey-Bass, 1996.

West, C., Farmer, J., and Wolff, P. *Instructional Design: Implications from Cognitive Science.* Upper Saddle River, N.J.: Prentice Hall, 1991.

Wiggins, G., and McTeghe, J. *Understanding by Design.* Alexandria, Va.: Association for Supervisors and Curriculum, 1998.

Zimmerman, B. J., Bonner, S., and Kovach, R. *Developing Self-Regulated Learners: Beyond Achievement to Self-Efficacy.* Washington, D.C.: American Psychological Association, 1996.

Index

A

Action learning, 58, 71
Action template, 157
Action timetable, 69
Active listening, 83
Administrators, 137, 138–139
Adolescent development: adapting course to, 95; challenges in, 2; and motivation, 95; personal identity in, 10, 11; tasks in, 2; transformation during, 10; transition during, 10
Adventure challenges, 42
Advisory groups, 97
Age, student, and stages of self-directed learning, 28
Alumni, use of, in assessment of self-directed learning, 119
Apprenticeships, 41
Aristotle, 64, 110
Assessment: in learning packages, 25; observations for, 92; of student-planned projects, 39; student-teacher conferences for, 130–131; tests for, 118, 119; use of alumni in, 119. *See also* Evaluation; Self-assessment
Attitudes: to boost self-directed learning, 161–162; during crisis, 103–104; development of, 44–45; effect on actions, 154–156; self-assessment of, 144–147; self-management of, 69–70. *See also* Emotions

B

Baker, S., 33
Bandura, A., 44–45
Baseline performance, 119, 120
Behavior. *See* Conduct
Bishop Carroll High School, 36
Bonner, S., 7
Brain research, 1, 7
Buckingham, M., 98
Butler, K., 62

C

Canadian Coalition of Self-Directed Learning, 36
Candy, P. C., 8
Career exploration challenges, 42
Celebrations, 81, 105, 130
Centennial School, 33
Challenges: achievement areas of, 41–42; adventure, 42; apprenticeships for, 41; benefits of, 98; career exploration, 42; competencies in, 40; creative expression, 41–42; definition of, 40, 80; difficulty of, 28, 29; encouragement during, 45; examples of, 41–42; logical inquiry, 41; and motivation, 97–98; outcome statements for, 15–16, 31, 33; overview of, 11–12; practical application, 41; proposals for, 41, 42; research on, 98; service, 42, 94; in student learning agreement, 79–80; trips for, 41
Chemainus High School, 33
Clarity, 154, 155
Clifton, D. O., 98
Coalition of Essential Schools, 36
Competence template, 157
Competencies: accurate assessment of, 123; in challenges, 40; expressing skills as, 71–72; outcomes for, 31, 32, 39–40; overview of, 39, 122–123
Conduct, 18, 106–108
Confidence, 154, 155
Constructivist theory, 8
Contracts. *See* Student learning agreement
Cooperative learning, 8, 17
Counseling approach, 104, 108
Coursework: adapting, to adolescent development, 95; creating outcomes for, 29–34; difficulty of, 28–29; learning episodes for, 46–47, 54–56; learning guides for, 15, 34–35, 36; learning packages for, 25–26, 34–37; negotiating credit for, 36; productivity in, 43, 44; and student readiness, 28–29; student-planned projects for, 38–39; tracking progress in, 90–92, 106

Creative expression challenges, 41–42
Crisis resolution, 101–106
Criteria for Excellence (Francis W. Parker Charter Essential School), 116, 118
Csikszentmihalyi, M., 57, 99
Curriculum: competencies in, 39–42; domains of, 10; inquiry-based, 60–61; linking outcomes to, 30; outcome statements for, 15; requirements of, 28

D

Decision making, 61–62, 63
Demonstrations: and emotions, 128, 129; examples of, 128–129; outcomes of, 128; overview of, 22, 126, 127–128; in student learning agreement, 81
Determination, 155
Dunlosky, J., 7

E

Emotions, 128, 129. *See also* Attitudes
Empowerment, 105, 137
Environment: expanding options for, 16–17, 18; overview of, 10–11; for productivity, 94; as self-directed learning principle, 10–11; for self-planned learning, 26; in traditional versus self-directed classroom, 16, 23
Erikson, E. H., 7
Evaluation: conferences for, 105; of current practice in self-directed learning, 142–143; of student-learning agreement, 81; for success, 99. *See also* Assessment
Expectations. *See* Outcomes
Experiences: benefits of, 47; creation of, 47–49; for difficult students, 108; dimensions of, 48; examples of, 46, 47, 54–55, 55–56, 152–153; and motivation, 94; new, 102–103; outcomes for, 31, 32; overview of, 10, 53; records of, 69; resources for, 18; as self-directed learning principle, 10; simulations of, 49; teachers' role in, 48, 53; trips as, 41
Experts, student, 99
Expression template, 158

F

Feedback, 27, 97
Feelings. *See* Emotions
Ford, M. E., 9, 96
Foster, R., 33
Francis W. Parker Charter Essential School, 60, 115–116
Freedoms, 106

G

Gallup study of strengths, 98
Gardner, H., 19
Generativity, 64
Goal setting: considering personal interests during, 96–97; and motivation, 96; for new experiences, 103; for student learning agreement, 78–79; for student-planned projects, 38–39
Graduation, 122, 123–124
Graesser, A., 7
Grant, S., 35

H

Hacker, D., 7
Hands-on learning. *See* Experiences
Hart, L. A., 7
Hatcher, M., 108
Hodgins, B., 108
Holistic Rubric (Francis W. Parker Charter Essential School), 116–117
Holt, J., 115
Hwa, C. L., 38

I

Identity, personal, 10
Importance statement, 78–79
Independent thinking: decision making in, 61–62, 63; development of, 18–19, 24–25, 58–64; example activity for, 62, 63; generativity for, 64; information gathering in, 61; investigations for, 25, 60–62; organizational process skills for, 68–72; outcomes for, 24; problem solving for, 64–65; process templates for, 65–68; relationship to questioning, 59–60; and teacher-directed learning, 59; teaching methods for, 24–25
Information gathering, 61, 67, 100
Inner states. *See* Attitudes
Inquiry-based curriculum, 60–61
Instructional materials, 16–18, 24, 41
Instructional options, 17
Interaction: for difficult students, 109; moving from lectures to, 45; in support groups, 163–165
Investigation: for independent thinking, 25, 60–62; overview of, 19; process of, 62, 63–64; relationship to questioning, 60; relationship to study, 50; skills in, 58, 60–62; template for, 66, 67–68
Island Pacific School, 38

J

James, W., 9
Jefferson County Open School, 6, 40, 95, 97, 109, 113, 124
Johnson, D. W., 8, 163
Johnson, R. T., 8, 163

K

Knowledge outcomes, 30, 32
Kolb, D. A., 48
Kovach, R., 7

L

Learning: approaches to, 170–171; control of, 11, 43; expanding options for, 16–18; natural drive for, 1, 9–10; as self-directed learning principle, 9–10; as social domain, 70; student management of, 12
Learning episodes, 46–47, 54–56
Learning guides, 15, 34–35, 36
Learning packages, 25–26, 34–37
Learning styles, 6
Lectures, 45
Lesson planning: and encouraging productivity, 51–52; and experience planning, 47–49; involving students

in, 52–54; learning episodes in, 46–47; principles of, 43–46; and promotion of study, 49–51
Letters of validation, 124, 127
Listening skills, 82–83, 104
Logical inquiry challenges, 41

M

MacVicar, R., 33
Masterwork, 38
McIntosh, D., 35
McRae, G., 37
McTeghe, J., 50, 59, 60
Mega-metacognition, 54
Memorization, 19
Mentors, 18, 97
Metacognition, 7, 54
Mission statements, 140–141
Model Schools Project (MSP), 36
Modeling, 94
Motivation: and adolescent development, 95; barriers to, 93; for challenges, 97–98; and conduct, 106–107; and crisis resolution, 101–106; of difficult students, 99, 106–109; and effect of nurturing environment, 94; encouraging, 95–99; and experiences, 94; and feedback, 97; and goal setting, 96; and identification of student strengths, 98; and introduction of self-directed learning, 93–94, 102; and mentors, 97; and modeling of self-directed learning, 94; and new experiences, 102–103; overview of, 12, 93; and personal interests, 96–97; principles of, 93–95; and reflection, 96; and student learning agreement, 20; and student readiness, 93; and success, 98–99; working journal for, 99–101
MSP. *See* Model Schools Project (MSP)
Myles, K., 95

N

Neve, C. D., 7

O

Oak Bay High School, 62
Observations, 92, 106
Openness, 155, 156
Optimism, 45
Organizational process skills, 68–72, 157–158
Outcomes: for challenges, 15–16, 31, 33; competency, 31, 32; defining, 15–16; of demonstrations, 128; examples of, 30–31, 32, 33, 34; experience, 31, 32; expressing competencies in, 39–40; for independent thinking, 24; knowledge, 30, 32; of learning packages, 34; linking curriculum to, 30; openness of, 30, 31–32; overview of, 29–30; planning approach to, 24; rubrics to clarify, 115; skills, 30, 32; specific versus general, 31–32; in student learning agreement, 78; task, 30, 32; and textbooks, 32; uses of, 33; writing statements for, 15, 24, 30

P

Packages. *See* Learning packages
Parents, 42, 130–131, 139

Passages: criteria for, 123; definition of, 40, 80, 123; introduction of, 40; process of, 148–151; in student learning agreement, 80
Personal domain, 10, 47, 70–71
Personal identity, 10
Personal Performance Profile, 113, 114, 115
Personal transition. *See* Transition
Phillips, G., 108
Plan section of student learning agreement, 79
Portfolios, 21, 121–122
Practical application challenges, 41
Presentations, 22, 130–131
Principal. *See* Administrators
Prior knowledge, 44
Problem solving: developing skills for, 64–65; reflection in, 64–65; strategy for, 65, 83–84; in student learning agreement, 80; in student-teacher conference, 83–84
Process templates, 65–68, 157–158
Process thinking: example of, 71; overview of, 57–58, 71; purpose of, 72; template for, 67
Productivity: aspects of, 52; benefits of, 51; emphasis on, 43–44; encouragement of, 51–52; examples of, 46, 47, 51, 55, 56, 152–153; nurturing environment for, 94; overview of, 53–54; process of, 52; relationship to study, 52; and skill development, 51; teachers' role in, 54; and working journal, 100
Professional development, 133, 134, 135
Proposals: for challenges, 41, 42; negotiation of, 42; overview of, 73; writing instructions for, 148–149. *See also* Student learning agreement
Psychosocial theory, 7–8

Q

Questioning: as framework for curriculum, 60–61; relationship to independent thinking, 59–60; relationship to investigations, 60; in student-teacher conference, 82; as study dimension, 50; using textbooks for, 59–60

R

Radom, J., 35, 37
Realism stage of crisis, 105
Recognition stage of crisis, 103–104
Reflection, 64–65, 96, 155, 156, 168–169
Reisman, D., 58–59
Research: on brain, 1, 7; on challenge, 98; effect on teaching methods, 6–9; on learning styles, 6; on metacognition, 7; on strengths, 98; supporting self-directed learning, 6–9, 135
Respect, 99
Reward. *See* Celebrations
Rubrics, 21, 115–118
Rules, classroom, 18, 107

S

Saint Paul Open School, 124, 125
Schedules, 139
SDL. *See* Self-directed learning (SDL)

Self-assessment: areas of, 112; and baseline performance, 119, 120; benefits of, 111; of competencies, 122–123; demonstrations for, 22, 126, 127–128; establishing criteria for, 111, 115, 119, 120; individualizing, 120–121; overview of, 12, 21, 110; of passages, 123; Personal Performance Profile for, 113, 114, 115; portfolios for, 21, 121–122; preparing students for, 112; presentations for, 22; process of, 21; purpose of, 110, 114; rubrics for, 21; of self-directed learning attitudes, 144–147; and student learning agreement, 20–21; of student readiness for self-directed learning, 144–147; teachers' use of, 110; transcripts for, 22, 110–111, 123–126; types of, 21–22; working journal for, 21–22. *See also* Assessment

Self-directed learning (SDL): barriers to, 160–161; benefits of, 6; course framework in, 27; development of, 14–22; elements of, 11–13; evaluation of current practice of, 142–143; framework for teaching 14–22; guidelines for, 159–160; importance of, 2–3; introduction of, 93–94, 102, 138; modeling of, 94; overview of, 2; planning steps for, 23–24; principles of, 9–11; research support for, 6–9, 135; stages in, 3, 24–28, 29; students' role in, 3, 4, 27; summary of, 133; versus teacher-directed learning, 2–3, 43–44, 45, 135–136; teachers' role in, 3–6, 27; teaching methods in, 5; transformation from teacher-directed learning to, 23–24, 29, 138–139

Self-directed learning school: administrative support for, 137, 138–139; benefits of, 136; purpose of, 136; schedules in, 139; sense of community in, 141; size of, 137; starting a, 137–138; teachers' role in, 137–138; vision for, 140–141

Self-efficacy, 2

Self-management: action timetable for, 69; of attitudes, 69–70; to avoid crisis, 103–104; instruction in, 70; and learning packages, 25–26, 34–37; overview of, 12; and pacing of activities, 25–26, 90–91; skills for, 69–70; in student learning agreement, 80

Self-planned learning, 26

Seligman, M.E.P., 45

Service challenges, 42, 94

Skill development, 57–72, 157–158; increasing complexity in, 44; in independent thinking, 19; investigation for, 19; memorization for, 19; overview of, 11, 18–19; process of, 19; and productivity, 51; for study, 50; in teacher-directed learning, 19

Skills: in action learning, 58; expressing, as competencies, 71–72; for information gathering, 61; in investigations, 58, 60–62; joining of, to create processes, 57–58; listening, 82–83, 104; organizational process, 68–72; overview of, 57; in personal domain, 70–71; for problem solving, 64–65; in process templates, 66, 157–158; for self-management, 69–70; in social domain, 70–71; for student-planned projects, 69–70. *See also specific skills*

Skills outcomes, 30, 32

Social domain, 10, 47, 70–71

Socrates, 64

Sprenger, M., 8

Stankowski, M., 108

Sternberg, R. J., 9

Strengthfinder.com, 98

Strengths, students', identification of, 98

Student learning agreement: celebrations in, 81; challenges in, 79–80; completion of, 21; demonstrations in, 81; evaluation measures in, 81; examples of, 74–77, 84–90; goal setting in, 78–79; importance statement in, 78–79; and motivation, 20; negotiation of, 20, 81–87; outcomes in, 78; outline of, 74; as outline of self-directed learning process, 77; overview of, 20, 73–74; passages in, 80; plan section in, 79; practice writing for, 87–88; problem solving in, 80; process of, 81; purpose of, 21; and self-assessment, 20–21; self-management in, 80; tracking progress in, 90–92. *See also* Proposals

Student-planned projects: assessment of, 39; frameworks for, 38; goal setting for, 38, 39; overview of, 38; planning process for, 39, 52–53; skills for, 69–70

Students: age of, and stages of self-directed learning, 28; attitudes of, 44–45, 69–70, 103–104; and control of learning, 11, 43; difficult, 106–109; emotions of, 128, 129; as experts, 99; identifying strengths of, 98; ranking of, 5; readiness of, for self-directed learning, 28, 44, 93, 144–147; role in student-directed learning, 3, 4, 27; strengths of, 98; support groups for, 163–165

Student-teacher conference: for assessment, 130–131; for difficult students, 108; examples of, 82, 83, 84; listening skills for, 82–83; overview of, 22; preparation for, 20; problem solving in, 83–84; purpose of, 81–82; questioning in, 82; teachers' role in, 81–82

Study: dimensions of, 50; examples of, 46, 47, 51, 55, 56, 152–153; overview of, 49, 53; process of, 49–50; relationship to investigation, 50; relationship to productivity, 52; skill development for, 50; teachers' role in, 53

Success, 98–99, 103–105

Superintendents. *See* Administrators

Support groups, 134, 163–165

Systems thinking, 71, 72

T

Task outcomes, 30, 32

Teacher-directed learning (TDL): and brain research, 7; content in, 43, 44; and control of learning, 11, 43; importance of, 2; and independent thinking, 59; learning episode example, 54–55; overview of, 2; versus self-directed learning, 2–3, 43–44, 45, 135–136; skill development in, 19; teachers' role in, 3; transformation from, to self-directed learning, 23–24, 29, 138–139

Teachers: and benefits of self-directed learning, 6; as counselors, 104, 108; effect of technology on, 5; and encouragement of independent thinking, 59; importance of, 132, 133; planning roles for, 24; preparing students for self-assessment, 112; professional development of, 133, 134, 135; role in experiences, 48; role in process templates, 68; role in self-directed learning, 3–6, 27; role in self-planned learning, 26; role in student-teacher conference, 82; role in teacher-directed learning, 3; in self-directed learning school start-up, 137–138; and support for learning packages, 35; support groups for, 134; use of self-assessment, 110; working journal for, 134

Teaching methods: effect of research on, 6–9; for group instruction, 17; for independent thinking, 24–25; for individual instruction, 17; in self-directed learning, 5; for whole-class instruction, 17

Teamwork template, 158

Technical domain, 10, 47

Technology, 5, 90–91

Tests, 118, 119

Textbooks, 32, 59–60

Thomas, E. C., 7

Thomas Haney High School, 35, 36, 90, 91, 119, 140

Tracking progress, 90–92, 106

Traditional classroom, 16, 23

Transcripts: contents of, 124; definition of, 22, 123–124; purpose of, 110–111

Transformation, adolescent, 7–8, 10, 107–108

Transitions, adolescent, 7–8, 10

Tremblay, R., 125–126, 127

Trips, 41

Trump, J. L., 36

Trump Plan, 36

V

Validation letters. *See* Letters of validation

Vision, 140–141

Vygotsky, L., 8

W

Wiggins, G., 50, 59, 60

Wilson, E. O., 48

Working journal: for crisis resolution, 105; example of, 166–169; and information gathering, 100; as motivational tool, 99–101; overview of, 21–22, 99–100; and productivity, 100; for teachers, 134; uses of, 100

Z

Zimmerman, B. J., 7

The Author

MAURICE GIBBONS, a professor emeritus in the Faculty of Education at Simon Fraser University, began his career as an elementary and secondary school teacher. He completed his B.A. at the University of British Columbia, his M.A. in English at the University of Washington, and his doctorate at Harvard University, where he was on the editorial board of the *Harvard Educational Review*. Among his more than sixty academic articles, the most celebrated are "Walkabout, Searching for the Right Passage from Childhood and School" (*Phi Delta Kappan*, 1974), and the follow-up article, "Walkabout Ten Years Later" (*Phi Delta Kappan*, 1984). Gibbons's books include Individualized Instruction: An Analysis of the Programs (Teachers' College Press), The New Secondary Education (Phi Delta Kappan) and The Walkabout Papers (Eduserve). He has also published textbooks, short stories, and poetry. The main focus of his work is on the development of educational programs, with an emphasis on self-directed learning. Gibbons is currently a writer and sculptor living on Bowen Island, British Columbia, with his wife, Leslie. His SDL Web site is www.mauricegibbons.ca.

Printed in the USA
CPSIA information can be obtained
at www.ICGtesting.com
LVHW070504021223
765401LV00008B/495

9 780787 959555